Charles A Smith

The Peaceful Classroom

Compassion and Cooperation: Activities for three to five-year-olds

Floris Books

Illustrated by Nancy L Downing

First published in 1993
by Gryphon House, Inc, Beltsville MD 20705
This British version edited by Mary Charrington
published in 1998 by Floris Books

British Library CIP Data available

ISBN 0-86315-277-5 ✓

Printed in Great Britain
by Redwood Books, Trowbridge Wilts

Contents

Age

4 Kindness

Preface

My first book, a textbook titled *Promoting the Social Development of Young Children*, was published in 1982. In addition to the typical academic fare found in any textbook, the book included 111 activities to promote body and sensory awareness, emotional development, affiliation, conflict resolution and kindness in young children. These activities, with their emphasis on how children's beliefs about themselves and others influence relationships, were based on my experience teaching young children at Purdue University, Bowling Green State University and Texas Tech University

Promoting the Social Development of Young Children went out of print in 1988. In 1991 I received a call from the Peace Corps who was interested in the book. The Peace Corps had recently established a programme in Romania to assist those working with abandoned or orphaned children living in large institutions. The new government was concerned about the emotional, social and moral development of these children who were growing up in difficult circumstances. Some Peace Corps volunteers felt my book would be of value in their work.

This call inspired me to revise and republish the material found in the original text. Instead of simply repackaging material, I wanted to make four significant improvements to strengthen the new book. Firstly, I would emphasize positive social behaviour. Activities for the textbook that focused exclusively on body and sensory awareness would not be included. The best activities on social development from the textbook would be retained.

Numerous additional activities would be created to expand on this core. Secondly, practising teachers would be the primary audience for the new book. Instead of theory and research, the new book would emphasize large and small group activities that could easily be implemented by teachers of young children. Thirdly, the format of the activities would be expanded to refer to picture books that complement the activities. Stories of friendship, compassion, cooperation and kindness are powerful tools for reaching a young child's mind and heart. Fourthly, every activity in the book would offer suggestions for involving parents in the educational programme.

Parental involvement is an important element in *The Peaceful Classroom*. Each of the 162 activities in this book include at least one suggestion for reaching out to parents. Each section begins with a letter to parents you can reprint or rewrite to introduce parents to what you hope to accomplish. I am looking forward to hearing about the innovative ways you reach out to parents including newsletters, notice boards or sending notes home with children.

I would also like to hear the stories you have about these activities and how children responded to your efforts to nurture friendship, compassion, cooperation and kindness. I too have stories to tell: about the two young boys in my class who were my 'seeing eye dogs' while I wore a blindfold; about the shy young girl who took me for a walk outside on another occasion when I was blindfolded; about the young boy with cerebral palsy who crawled across the floor to reach and hug a classmate whose affection had just been rejected by another. Write to me care of the publisher if you are interested in sharing your experiences in *The Peaceful Classroom.*

Although I have assumed much different responsibilities since the original textbook was written, my heart will always be in the classroom, on the floor with young children, telling stories, giving puppet shows, talking, hugging, laughing. To these and all the other children who taught me about kindness, I extend a sincere thank you. I would also like to thank those teachers who participated in my university courses and workshops and whose enthusiasm and dedication inspired my efforts. I especially appreciate the support and insights provided by my friends Lois Bates, a day care teacher and Andrea Scheib, a home day care provider. Thanks also to Carolyn Foat, Bill Carver, Sue Morrow, Anne Ahlenius and Kitty Beverly, all exceptional teachers who touched my life over the years.

I would also like to express my appreciation to the professionals at Gryphon House, especially Larry Rood and Kathy Charner, for their guidance and enthusiasm. Finally, I owe a debt of kindness to my family: Betsy, Sarah and Bill for the chorus of support I needed to complete this project.

Introduction

Young children are ready and willing to learn, and teachers want to provide a quality educational programme that inspires them to create, discover and achieve.

However, the best educational programmes do more than just teach children how to count and say the alphabet. They should reach children's hearts as well as their minds. Self-esteem and effective relationships are important goals for this programme.

The Peaceful Classroom aims to help teachers make a real difference to children's lives. Each child should feel a part of the school group, make friends and play cooperatively with others. This programme will help them learn about basic human emotions such as happiness, sadness, anger and fear, and will encourage the children to respond compassionately to others during emotionally difficult moments. Hopefully they will also learn to treat others with respect and gentleness, to be generous and to offer help when possible.

Success depends on establishing an effective partnership between home and school. Keep parents informed of their children's progress and suggest activities that they can do at home to provide continuity with what is being done at school.

Teachers of young children are at the beginning of the wonderful lifelong enterprise of nurturing a human spirit. What we do has the potential to endure over time, long after a child has left our care.

Do you remember the first time a child called you 'teacher'? How did you react? Were you surprised? Were you proud? 'Teacher!' a child declared, and the whole world changed for us. At this moment we became someone who had power and magic in the eyes of a young child. With such power came the responsibility to provide the best for children entrusted in our care. We became a companion and advocate for children in their learning journey. We became real teachers, not just childminders or playground monitors.

Real teachers do more than fill children's heads with numbers, shapes and letters of the alphabet. These skills are important. But real teachers change lives. To change lives, we have to reach out to children's hearts as well as their minds. We have to create a place of safety where children are free to investigate the world around them, to discover their inner landscape of emotions and to explore human relationships. By emphasizing non-violence, compassion and the understanding of our shared humanity, we create *The Peaceful Classroom*.

We can use spontaneous opportunities to help children understand themselves and others. A bird feeding its young, two armies of ants locked in combat, a child with a grazed knee are opportunities to learn about life and the human condition. We can also encourage children to explore the give-and-take nature of human contact during free play. As they experience this social laboratory, children learn about the consequences of compassion and cruelty, cooperation and competition.

We can also create and introduce planned experiences in the reception classroom or nursery and in small groups. In these more structured situations, we can teach children the skills that will enable them to live peacefully and productively with others. Group experiences provide a safe context for children to observe, try out new skills and practise what they have learned.

By weaving planned activities with more spontaneous encounters, we can create a powerful and responsive learning environment that encourages friendship, compassion, cooperation and kindness in young children.

About *The Peaceful Classroom*

The Peaceful Classroom provides 162 classroom activities for children from about three to five years of age, although they can be used with children up to age eight. Activities are organized into four chapters: Friendship, Compassion, Cooperation and Kindness. Each chapter explores three or more skills:
Friendship: association, conversation, belonging, friendship
Compassion: recognition of emotions, problem solving, expression
Cooperation: cooperation, consideration for others, negotiation
Kindness: looking after people/things, gentleness, helping, generosity, rescue/protection, respect/encouragement

Each of the four themes build upon each other, providing a foundation for those that follow. In general, Friendship activities provide a foundation for Compassion, Cooperation and Kindness.

Within each chapter, activities focusing on one skill prepare children for those that follow. For example, association activities should generally precede those focusing on belonging.

In addition, activities within each chapter are listed in the order of age complexity, beginning with those appropriate for three year olds and older and concluding with those for five year olds and older.

There are many ways to use this book. One way is to do all the activities in the book developmentally appropriate for your children. Start with the first activity in the Friendship chapter, then continue in sequence until the activities become too difficult. Then move to the first activity in the second chapter, Compassion, and continue as before until the activities become too difficult. Repeat with the chapter on Cooperation and finish with Kindness. This strategy provides the greatest scope over the longest period of time.

Another approach is to choose activities for a specific skill like gentleness or association. There is a list of activities for each of the sixteen skills beginning on page twenty. Activities for any single skill are often found in more than one chapter.

Designing your own strategy is always a good way to proceed. If you have a specific issue in mind and a limited amount of time, you can choose and introduce activities in a developmentally appropriate sequence. If you teach three year olds, for example, and want to focus on 'appreciation and respect for the environment,' you could do the following activities:

GROWING FLOWERS
PLANT LIFE
ADOPT A TREE
NATURE TRIBUTE
BIRD DINNER
CLASS TREE
CLASS NATURE COLLAGE

You can assemble activities around such issues as sensitivity for disabled people and celebration of racial and ethnic diversity. The basic skills of friendship, compassion, cooperation and kindness can be combined in various ways to address nearly any social issue of concern to you and the children's parents.

How Activities Are Structured

SKILLS
The specific skill or skills targeted by the activity are listed in the top right corner of the activity description.

PLACE
The location suggested for the activity is indicated by a symbol in the top right corner of the page:

○ Circle
✄ Art area
✢ Science area
❦ Kitchen
❀ Open space
✳ Outside
⌂ Inside

Where more than one is listed, the children move from one to another in the order listed.

AGE
The minimum age for the activity is also given in the top right corner. This is only a baseline. Older children should begin with the simpler activities, gradually leading up to the maximum for their age.

THINGS YOU WILL NEED
A list of materials you will need to accomplish the activity successfully. In every case, the materials should be readily available or simple to prepare.

INTRODUCTION
Following 'Things you will need' there is a small amount of background information regarding the skills and suggestions for implementing the activity.

WHAT TO DO
A step-by-step explanation of how to introduce and complete the activity. Suggestions as to what a teacher might say and do are provided. Consider this section as an illustration of the intent and approach of the experience. How you actually implement the activity should reflect your own unique style as a teacher.

WANT TO DO MORE?
Whenever possible, this section comments on the activity's limitations or strengths and suggests ways to make it more successful. Many activities can be made simpler for younger children or more challenging for older ones.

This section may also include a recommended children's book related to the activity's general theme. In addition to reading the book in your classroom, you can recommend it to parents for reading at home.

INVOLVING PARENTS
The best educational programmes create a partnership between teachers and parents. An Overview is provided at the beginning of each chapter. Use these overviews as a guide to explain your emphasis on friendship, compassion, cooperation or kindness to parents. Every activity also includes a brief suggestion for involving parents in the education of their children. You can give these suggestions to parents when they pick their children up at the end of the school day, or prepare a sheet of instructions for them.

Suggestions for success

Are you happy about the activity?
Activities should make sense to you as the teacher. You should be comfortable with what you select. If you feel uncomfortable about introducing an activity, choose another.

Is the activity suitable for your group?
Activities should meet the needs and interests of the group and individual children. At the beginning of the year, 'name' games are useful since children may want to get to know each other better. Some activities may be too threatening or confusing to children early in the year when they are still strangers.

Can you blend activities together?
Different types of activities can be used in conjunction with each other to increase their impact. To emphasize cooperation, read a story about two children working together, organize cooperative painting, and lead the children in a cooperative fingerplay. Look for different ways to blend the activities you do in your classroom.

How do you sequence your activities?
The activities in this book are listed in their approximate order of complexity. Keep in mind that children may respond better to some activities if they have been properly prepared by one or more previous activities. BLIND KIND, for example, should be preceded by I CANNOT SEE and KNOW SEE, both of which prepare children to wear blindfolds.

Are the children ready for the activity?
Children should never be physically or psychologically pressurized to participate. They are likely to become involved willingly if they know what to do, and you are prepared and enthusiastic. Sometimes a group may be ready, but individual children may be unwilling to participate. If so, be prepared to direct them to another supervised activity away from the main group.

Is it going according to plan?
Your effectiveness as a leader depends on your ability to adjust as the activity unfolds. Children may react unpredictably, or an unexpected learning opportunity might occur. Be ready to adjust your activity plan spontaneously to overcome problems or to take advantage of favourable circumstances.

Is the classroom safe?
The well-being of the children should be your highest priority in everything you do. Every safety precaution should be taken as you invite children to participate in classroom activities. Eliminate hazards like sharp objects if you involve children in action games or movement. Supervise the use of scissors during craft activities. Be vigilant whenever blindfolds are used. Remain alert to these and other potential problems and observant of every child in your group.

Friendship skills, definitions and examples

ASSOCIATION
Recognizes others who belong to the school or nursery group.
Example:
• *Anna and Zoe go to my school.*

CONVERSATION
Attracts and holds the attention of others in socially acceptable ways; Engages in positive conversations with peers.
Examples:
• A child taps another child on the shoulder and asks her a question when she turns around.

- *Hello, Jamie. Would you give me the crayons?*
- *Emily, come and play 'trucks' with us.*

BELONGING

Identifies relationships within their primary family group;
understands why families are important; expands their sense of belonging to include groups other than their immediate families;
forms a group identity that embraces everyone in the group; uses the terms us and our to refer to the entire group; will lead and follow others in the group; recognizes when someone is absent from the group.
Examples:
- *My daddy's name is David, my mummy's name is Cathy and my sister's name is Sarah. We are a family. Families are important because the mummies and daddies feed their babies.*
- *Forest School is my school, and this is my class, and Mrs. Penner is my teacher.*
- *Everyone here is in Mrs. Wilson's class. She is our teacher.*
- *Teacher, where is Cindy? She's not here today.*

FRIENDSHIP

Get to know and be known by other individuals in more personal ways.
Examples:
- *Mark really likes chocolate cake. I like orange cake.*

Compassion skills, definitions and examples

RECOGNITION OF EMOTIONS

Uses visual and auditory cues to recognize happiness, fear, sadness and anger.
Example:
- A three-year-old points to another child who is crying and says to his mother, *He sad.*

PROBLEM SOLVING

Describes happiness, sadness, fear and anger; identifies circumstances that affect emotions, the consequences of emotional behaviour and effective ways to express their own emotions and respond to the emotions of others.
Examples:
- A five-year-old describes sadness as feeling like ...*there are tears in your heart.*
- A four-year-old says, *When I feel sad, sometimes I cry.*
- A seven-year-old comments, *When you get angry, it doesn't do any good to hit—they might hit you back.*

EXPRESSION

Finds words to describe their own emotional experiences;
responds emotionally to loss, danger, frustration and gain; responds to their own emotions with effective, compassionate action.
Examples:
- While watching a television show, a three-year-old runs to her mother and says, *I scared, mummy.*
- When he finds his pet canary dead in its cage, a four-year-old cries.
- When he starts to get scared watching television, a five-year-old leaves to play in his room.

Cooperation skills, definitions and examples

COOPERATION

Understands the word 'cooperation;' works together with others to solve a problem or reach a common goal; understands that actions are interrelated and are mutually beneficial.
Examples:
- *Look, teacher, Terry and I are cooperating!*
- Three children work together to clean up an activity area.

CONSIDERATION OF OTHERS
Makes adjustments in behaviour to
accommodate another person; shows
awareness of another person's goals.
Examples:
- Child moves over at a crowded table
  to make room for another.
- Child runs slower to let a partner
  catch up.

NEGOTIATION
Makes suggestions for preventing or
resolving a conflict; describes
consequences of another's behaviour;
Describes circumstances surrounding a
conflict.
Examples:
- *We all want the balloon. So let's take
  turns.*
- *Michael, if you play so roughly
  somebody might get hurt.*
- *They are fighting because Rebecca
  took his truck.*

Kindness skills, definitions and examples

LOOKING AFTER OTHERS
Understands the basic needs of plants,
animals and people; learns simple steps
for nurturing the growth of plants,
animals and people; understands well,
ill, hurt and taking care of; describes
steps for restoring health following
illness or accident; Learns simple skills
for easing distress and restoring health.
Examples:
- *Flowers need water to grow.*
- A child feeds her pet hamster every
  day.
- *Teacher, my tummy hurts and I feel
  sick.*
- *When you are ill, your mummy takes
  care of you.*
- *When you are ill, you stay in bed and
  eat soup until you are better.*
- A child prepares a tray of crackers
  and orange juice for her sick mother.

GENTLENESS
Understands the harmful consequences
of careless or aggressive behaviour
toward the environment, plants, animals
and people; treats the environment,
plants, animals and people with respect
and tenderness.
Examples:
- A child carefully holds a guinea pig in
  his arms, avoiding sudden or
  squeezing movements.
- A child in the nursery gently puts his
  arm around a crying classmate to
  comfort her after she falls down.

HELPING
Can identify how to help someone solve
a problem; assists another to achieve his
or her goal; expresses appreciation to
others.
Examples:
- *If Jamie can't reach the shelf, I can
  get it for him because I am taller.*
- *Here, Miss Brown, I can help you
  pick up the crayons you dropped.*
- *Thanks for your help, Sandy.*

GENEROSITY
Differentiates between mine, yours and
ours; derives satisfaction from owner-
ship; feels secure about their belongings;
makes sacrifices by giving what they
own to someone in need;
Examples:
- *Don't take that truck. It's mine. I
  brought it from home.*
- A child takes her friend to her room
  and says, *Look Katie, all these toys on
  this shelf are mine. Everything over
  there belongs to my sister.*
- A child gives his friend one of his
  biscuits and says, *Here Mark. You
  haven't got any biscuits so I will give
  you this one.*

RESCUE/PROTECTION

Can differentiate between safe and dangerous activities; removes threats to the safety of another person; can think of effective strategies to prevent harm to the environment, plants, animals and people; intervenes, when possible, to prevent harm to the environment, plants, animals and people.

Examples:

- *Matches are dangerous. They can burn you.*
- A child removes a pin he sees on the floor so that his baby brother will not hurt himself.
- *You stay safe by playing in the front yard and not going out in the street. A car could hit you in the street.*
- While playing on swings in the park, a kindergartner tells two first graders to stop teasing her younger brother.

RESPECT/ENCOURAGEMENT

To esteem the environment, plants, animals and people; motivates others to reach a goal; shows pleasure with the accomplishments of others.

Examples:

- *Miss Brown, Isn't the tree beautiful?*
- *Come on Sunita, you can do it!*
- *Wow, Marcia. You're a really good runner!*

Recommended Reading

Fry-Miller, K. and Myers-Walls, J. *Young Peacemaker's Project Book*. (Elgin, IL: Bretheren Press, 1988.)

Johnson, D.W. and Johnson, R.T. *Learning Together and Alone: Cooperative, Competitive and Individualistic Learning*. (Allyn and Bacon 1994)

Orlick, T. *The Cooperative Sports and Games Book: Challenge without Competition* (Random House 1978.)

Prutzman, P., Burger, M.L., Bodenhamer, G., and Stern, L. *The Friendly Classroom for a Small Planet*. (New Society Publishers,US.)

Rubin, Z. *Children's Friendships*. (Open Books Pub.)

Schulman, M. *The Passionate Mind: Bringing Up an Intelligent and Creative Child*. (The Free Press, US, 1991.)

Wuthnow, R. *Acts of Compassion: Caring for Others and Helping Ourselves*. (Princeton University Press, 1991.)

Chapter One

Belonging and Friendship

○ Circle; ✂ Art; ❧ Science; ♨ Kitchen; ❀ Open space; ✳ Outside; △ Inside

Overview

The Peaceful Classroom's first emphasis is on belonging and friendship. Help the children learn the following:

> The names of other children in the class.
> How to attract and hold the attention of others in a pleasant way.
> That they are an important part of the school group.
> How to invite each other to play and make friends.
> How families are different and why they are important.

Use words like 'names,' 'class,' 'group' and 'belonging.' Children will participate in activities like NAME CHANTING, CLASS MOBILE, MAGNET and ROBOT CLASS. It is also a good idea to read carefully selected picture books that focus on belonging and friendship.

Children with high self-esteem are aware that they belong. They feel nurtured and accepted by others. They reach out self-confidently because they believe they can contribute. Skills in this area provide a foundation that can be built on. The emphasis now on belonging and friendship will complement all other areas of this educational programme.

There are many ways in which parents and teachers can work together to nurture children's talents for making friends. One of the most important things is to share memories with the children. Also, many of the school activities can be tried at home.

Name Chanting

Association   Age $3+$ ○

Things you will need
Nothing

All children love to hear their name spoken by others. As they listen and clap in unison to the beat of each other's names, they begin to develop a sense of community. Do not use phrases that might embarrass a child. Begin the activity with your own name.

What to do
1. Make up a brief rhyme for each child's name (nonsense rhymes are fine). For example:
    Anne, Anne, bought a pan.
    Peter, Peter, pumpkin eater.
    Sarah, Sarah, fe fo farah.
    Bill, Bill, climbed a hill.

2. Slowly chant each rhyme twice and clap your hands to the beat of each word, for example: *Peter, Peter,* (two claps) *pumpkin eater* (two claps).

3. Look directly at the child whose name is being chanted. The speed of the chant and clapping can be varied.

Want to do more?
You can ask older children to think of words that rhyme with their names, for example, Mike/bike. Another child or the teacher then makes up a chant for the group to repeat. For example, *Mike, Mike, rides a bike.* Or dispense with the rhyme altogether. Ask a child to name something she likes to eat and make up a rhythmic chant incorporating her preference, for example:
    Sarah, Sarah,
    loves ice cream.
• Read *George and Martha One Fine Day* by James Marshall (Houghton Mifflin).

Involving parents
Suggest to parents that they try this activity at home with their children. Name rhyming might be especially fun while travelling in the car.

Roll Over   ○

Association, cooperation   Age *3+*

Things you will need
One medium-sized rubber or foam ball

Gathering in a circle is a great way to build a sense of group identity among children. Adding a song or chant increases the feeling of togetherness. Even a simple activity like rolling a ball back and forth calls for the give-and-take necessary for getting on well with others.

What to do
1. Form a circle with the children standing and ask them to hold each other's hands gently. Ask them to chant with you:
   Hands together,
   Hands together, make a group,
   (Join hands)
   Hands together, make a group,
   All together, here we stand, *(Hands now joined)*
   This is our group, so lend a hand. *(Raise joined hands)*

2. Bring the children in so that the circle is tighter and ask everyone to sit down. Take out the ball and tell the children you will slowly roll it to someone opposite you. When that person catches the ball, everyone in the group should say their name in unison. That person then rolls the ball to someone else. Continue until everyone has been named. Repeats are acceptable as long as everyone is named at least once.

Want to do more?
Create and practise a melody for the chant.
• With older children, the child who catches the ball can name the child who rolled it.

• Introduce last names or name an item of clothing worn by one or more of the children. A child then rolls the ball to the child who has been named or who is wearing the relevant clothing.
• The *Hands Together* chant can be used any time you form a circle.
• Read *One, Two ...Where's the Shoe?* by Richard Rosenstein, illustrated by Victor Ambrus (Floris Books).

Involving parents
Encourage parents to talk about their childhood friends with their children. What did their friends look like? What did they enjoy doing with them? Parents can draw a picture of a childhood friend and ask their children to do the same. They might like to stick up both pictures, for example, in the kitchen.

Child in the Den

Association   Age **3+**

Things you will need
Nothing

This activity is patterned after the traditional game of THE FARMER'S IN HIS DEN, substituting children's names for farmer, wife, nurse and so on. If you have more than ten to twelve children, you might consider stopping after about half the children have been selected. The activity can be repeated later that day or the next to include those not named. You may also divide the children into two groups if another adult is available.

What to do
1. The group forms a standing circle, and one child is selected to begin. This child goes to the centre of the circle, and others sing while they move in a circle around her. For example:
   Sarah's in the den,
   Sarah's in the den.
   Ee ay ally oh
   Sarah's in the den.

2. The song continues in its familiar manner with the named child pointing to another. For example:
   Sarah picks Michael,
   Sarah picks Michael.
   Ee ay ally oh,
   Sarah picks Michael.

3. When there is only one child left they stand alone while the others return to the group.
   Tom stands alone,
   Tom stands alone.
   Ee ay ally oh,
   Tom stands alone.

Want to do more?
Try reversing the rules by starting with everyone clustered together in the centre of what will become a circle. The first child skips around the group while the rest of the children chant. From the outside of the group, the first child points to another child. When the chant is completed, they join hands. Gradually a circle will form around the remaining children. The final verse ('stands alone') is omitted.
• Read *The Mouse and the Potato,* by Thomas Berger illustrated by Carla Grillis (Floris Books).

Involving parents
Prepare a short descriptive list of the children in your group, naming each child and giving addresses and phone numbers (with permission). With four-year-olds and older, briefly interview each child: What do you like to eat? What is your favourite toy? What do you like to watch on television? Include the replies for each child. Parents can go over this class list with their children at home.

Name Fame

Association   Age *3+*

Things you will need
Nothing

Naming activities are easier when the entire group participates simultaneously. Once children are more familiar with each other's names, they are more likely to be confident enough to respond alone.

What to do
1. Ask the children to stand in a circle holding hands . Move around inside the circle while everyone chants:
    Think hard, think hard,
    We hope we don't miss.
    Think hard, think hard,
    Now who is THIS?

2. Just before the word 'THIS,' stop and stand directly in front of one child. After the chant is finished, the group shouts the child's name in unison. This procedure can be repeated until everyone has been named.

3. Once they are familiar with the rules of the game, children can take turns making the selections.

Want to do more?
Make the activity more difficult by choosing a child to go around the circle from child to child during the chant. On 'THIS,' the moving child stops and has to name the child she is facing.
• Read *Jenny's Bear* by Michael Ratnett, illustrated by (Red Fox).

Involving parents
Encourage parents to invite their children to make a picture to send to one of their friends on the class list. Use the class list to address the envelope. Try to ensure that each child will receive a picture so that no one feels left out.

Class Mobile
Association, belonging

Age **3+**

○

Things you will need
One photograph of each child and teacher in the group
One hole punch
Various lengths of thread, one for each picture
One coat hanger

Some parents may be unable to obtain pictures of their children. If you think there might be a problem, borrow a Polaroid camera to take pictures at school. Polaroid pictures establish some consistency in quality and ensure that all children are included.

What to do
1. Before class starts, obtain photos of similar size for each child in your group. Punch a hole in the middle at the top of each picture. Tie one end of a single piece of thread through this hole. Suspend the coat hanger from the ceiling near where the group will meet.

2. Call the children together and invite them to help you make a CLASS MOBILE to hang in the classroom for all to see. The mobile will consist of photos of everyone who belongs to the group. Ask one child to name everyone in the group.

3. Take out the pictures and ask the group to name each person whose photo you hold up. Tie the pictures to the hanger at different heights. When finished, encourage children to comment on the activity. Hang the mobile somewhere where everyone can see it.

Want to do more?
The children can draw self-portraits on large index cards. Hole punch the cards and hang them with thread as you did the photos.

Involving parents
Parents can make a similar FAMILY MOBILE at home, using photos or self-portraits.

Magnet   ◯

Association, gentleness   Age 3+

Things you will need
Nothing

Ask children to be gentle when they touch the 'magnet.' Try the variation under Want to do more? with children who dislike the physical attention this activity involves.

What to do
1. Ask the children to join hands in a circle. When the music begins, the group skips or walks around while continuing to hold hands. When the music stops, call out a child's name. Everyone immediately breaks hands and runs to surround and gently touch the named child (the magnet).

2. As soon as the last child makes contact, begin the music again. Everyone joins hands in a circle and repeats the activity.

3. Continue until all the children have been named.

Want to do more?
Instead of touching the child, the rest of the children can join hands around them, chanting:

> Hello *(name)*, hello *(name)*. How
> are you? How are you?
> Hello *(name)*, hello *(name)*. We
> like you too!

Immediately after the chant, begin the music again and repeat the activity.
• Read *Kitten Finds a Home*, by Michele Coxon (Happy Cat).

Involving parents
Parents can help their child 'write' a note to send to one of their classmates. Older children can invent their own spelling, and younger children can dictate what they want to say. The children can also decorate the envelope, stick on a stamp and post the letter.

Class Tree

Belonging, cooperation

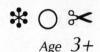

Age *3+*

Things you will need
Several colours of construction paper
Scissors
Crayons
Length of string for each child
Tape (or stapler)
Large branch
Bucket and sand
Large sheet of lining paper

This activity provides an excellent opportunity to emphasize the importance of treating nature with respect. Point out to children that the branch was no longer useful to the tree. Taking a branch from a live tree would not be the right thing to do.

What to do
1. Find a suitably large branch on the ground in a wooded area. (Take the children with you, if possible.) Strip all the dead leaves from the branch and insert the base into a bucket of sand for support.

2. Gather the children around the 'tree' and ask them if they think something is missing (leaves). Suggest they make some pretend leaves for the tree from pictures of their hands. Invite the children to go to the art area where construction paper and other materials are available.

3. Trace around the children's hands, using as many colours of construction paper as possible. Ask them to cut their 'hands' out and write their names on one side. Tape a piece of string to the middle finger of each paper hand.

4. Assemble the children with their cut-outs in a circle around the tree. Ask the children to hold up their leaves. As they do so, say something like, *All the leaves belong to the tree, and all of you belong to this class. Each leaf is important to the tree, and each of you is special to this class.* Ask each child to stand, one at a time, and select a place on the branch to tie their cut-out hand. Help, if necessary.

5. Find a safe place for the tree, where it is clearly visible but well out of harm's way.

Want to do more?
Instead of finding a real branch, paint a tree on a large piece of lining paper and tape it to a wall or notice board. Each child can put one hand in finger-paint — spread on a separate sheet of paper — and make an impression on one branch of the tree.
• Consider using other materials to represent the children: photos, ribbons, footprints, etc.
• Read *The Tree that Grew through the Roof* by Thomas Berger, illustrated by Marjan van Zeyl (Floris Books).

Involving parents
Show parents your class creation and suggest they make a similar FAMILY TREE at home.

Our Group

Belonging

✂ ○

Age *3+*

Things you will need
For each child:
One empty rectangular cardboard box, for example a tissue box
Two or three small stones that will fit inside the box
One 15 cm (6") paper plate
Tape
Crayons
Glue
Scissors
Construction paper and other decorative materials

The presence of a set of dolls representing children in the class reassures every child that he or she is an important part of the group.

What to do
1. Set materials out at the art table. Ask each child to draw a picture of his face on his paper plate. Place the stones inside each box. If the box has a lid tape this on. If the box has no lid stick tape across the open side to prevent the stones falling out. The stones should weight the bottom of the box when it is set on end. Glue the centre of the paper plate to end of the base of the box. The children can then decorate their 'figure' with clothes made of construction paper and other decorative materials. They can also add legs, taping them to the bottom end of the box.

2. When all the figures are completed, ask the children to bring them and come and sit in a circle near a suitably long shelf. Invite the children, one at a time, to place their figures on the shelf. When all the figures have been placed, say something like, *Here is our class, our group. Here is each one of us. Every day, when we first meet at the beginning of class, we will use these figures to help us remember who is in our group. You may take your figure back to the art area to make different clothes, but do not take anyone else's figure.*

3. Each morning, you can ask the children to take and hold their figures when they first meet as a group. The remaining figures will remind the children of who is absent.

Want to do more?
Other types of figures can be made. For example, a styrofoam ball can be decorated and glued to a tall plastic bottle.
• Older children can shade the paper plate to approximate their skin colour.
• Read *Thud!* by Nick Butterworth (HarperCollins).

Involving parents
Parents and children can make a similar set of 'dolls' at home and display the doll family in a special place.

Name Game
Association

○
Age 4+

Things you will need
Nothing

Rhythmic chanting and clapping can be used to help children learn each other's names early in the school year. Maintain a relatively fast tempo throughout this activity.

What to do
1. Begin with the naming chant and ask the group to repeat it with you. In this example, a teacher named Ann selects Hannah to begin.

   Ann, Ann, look at everyone —
   Point to Hannah, and then you're done.

2. After pointing to Hannah, the teacher asks Hannah to find Bill.

   Hannah, Hannah, look at everyone — Point to Bill, and then you're done.

3. Now Bill becomes the pointer. The activity continues until all children have been named. The last child can be asked to point at the teacher to complete the activity.

Want to do more?
For added interest, make simple construction paper flowers for each child. Instead of simply pointing, the selected child can approach and give the named child a flower.
• Children's names can also be placed in a container passed around the circle. Each child draws a name and announces it for the chant. The teacher begins, and from then on, the last child named becomes the 'pointer.'

Involving parents
Children can dictate to their parents a brief letter to one of their friends in the class. They can also decorate both the letter and the envelope before sending them.

Musical Names

Association   *Age* **4+**

Things you will need
Music
A chair for each child minus one

In this variation of musical chairs, everyone remains in the game. Regular musical chairs can distress children who are forced to leave the game and watch from the sidelines. All children like to hear others mention their name. Play the game several times to give everyone an opportunity.

What to do
1. Arrange the chairs in a circle. When the music stops, the child who cannot find a chair stands behind someone seated in the circle. Once everyone is positioned, the standing child names their seated partner.

2. In each successive round, remove a chair. After the halfway point, two or more children will be standing behind each seated child. Each of the standing children should say the seated child's name, one after the other.

3. At the end of the game, one seated child will be named by the rest of the group.

Want to do more?
For variety, reverse the movement of chairs: start with one, then add one each turn.

Involving parents
Encourage parents to arrange with the parents of one of their child's classmates for the children to visit after school or at the weekend. Parents should involve the children in planning activities for the visit.

Robot Class

Belonging, cooperation

◯ ✂

Age **4+**

Things you will need
Crayons
Paint
Large sheets of lining paper
Tape or stapler
Scissors

Make several different ROBOT CLASSES if there are more than ten children in your group. Arrange them side-by-side.

What to do
1. When you have gathered the children together tell them you would like to give them the opportunity to work together to make a very special 'paper person.' Tell them that this person will be composed of drawings of everyone in the class. The children decide which part of the body they would like to be. One child can be the left hand, another the right foot, another the head and so on.

2. Ask each child to lie on the lining paper so you can draw an outline of the chosen body part. Ask the children to cut out their names and put them on their parts of the body for the Robot Class. The children can decorate each part with paint or crayons. The parts of the body should then be taped or stapled together to hang up on the wall.

3. Use the occasion to discuss the range of physical differences among children in the class.

Want to do more?
Glue the parts of the body onto styrofoam and then glue the pieces together to make 'Robot statues.'
• Read *Leon and Bob* by Simon James (Walker Books).

Involving parents
Send home a length of lining paper so parents and children can make their own ROBOT FAMILIES.

No Words   ◯

Conversation   Age **4+**

Things you will need
Nothing

Young children are very egocentric and often have difficulty understanding the implications of a disability they cannot see. This activity will help them appreciate the importance of the senses in communication.

What to do
1. Prepare sign language that you can teach your children to represent simple words:

    I *(point to yourself)*,
    like *(hug yourself)*,
    help *(cup hands together)*
    eat *(bring hand to mouth)*,
    see *(cup hand over eyes)*,
    you *(point to child)*
    this *(point to object)*,
    daddy *(stroke imaginary beard)*,
    mummy *(stroke imaginary long hair)*

2. Talk with the children for a few moments about deafness. *Do you know, some people cannot hear. When the birds sing, they cannot hear their music; when lightning flashes in the sky, they cannot hear the thunder....* Continue with your own examples.

3. Take a moment just to listen quietly to nearby sounds. Emphasize that a deaf person cannot hear these sounds. *But even though they cannot hear what you say, many deaf people learn what's called sign language, a way to talk using your hands. I have made up some words for my hands. Watch what I do with my hands and tell me what I'm trying to say to you.*

4. Choose a very simple statement to act out, for example, *I see you.* (Point to yourself, then to your eyes, then to a child.)

5. Ask the children to tell you what they think you are trying to communicate. Go over each word one at a time. Invite the children to repeat your actions as you do them.

6. Add a few more words to your shared vocabulary. Combine the actions in three-word sentences and ask them to guess their meaning.

7. Invite the children to make up their own sentences.

8. After you have about nine words in your vocabulary, ask the children to create actions to represent additional words.

Want to do more?
Increase the complexity of this activity by expanding the vocabulary and increasing the number of actions in a statement.
• Emphasize that what the children are learning is not the official language deaf people use to sign. Invite a deaf person who knows how to sign to your class to talk with the children.

Involving parents
Describe the activity to parents and keep them informed of the words you are learning. Encourage them to use sign language in conversations at home. Parents may be able to suggest other actions to represent words that children can teach the group at school.

School Garden

Belonging, cooperation

✂ ○

Age **4+**

Things you will need
A large sheet of lining paper
Several colours of construction paper
Scissors
Crayons
Glue or paste

A garden is a good metaphor for a group. Each flower is separate and beautiful yet contributes to the loveliness of the whole. Although young children are not likely to understand the connection between metaphor and reality, working together to make a common product, and visibly demonstrating their togetherness makes this type of activity important.

What to do
1. Using different colours of construction paper, cut out a variety of stems, leaves and simple flower shapes.

2. Spread the lining paper across the table and set out the parts of the plants. With the children's assistance, draw the 'ground' for the class garden across the length of the paper.

3. Starting at one end of the sheet, assemble your flowering plant from the cut-outs by pasting them to the 'ground' on the lining paper. Write your name inside your flower. The children then take turns assembling and adding their flowers to the class garden. Each child's name should appear somewhere on their flower.

4. After all the flowers are assembled, invite the children to draw a sun, clouds, birds, insects and butterflies in the garden.

5. Once completed, the garden can be taped to a wall or tacked to a wide notice board.

6. Within the next few days, gather in a circle near the garden. Emphasize that just as each flower in a garden is special, so each child in the class is special. Point out the uniqueness of each flower.

Want to do more?
The children can cut out the stems, leaves and flowers themselves if they are old enough to manipulate the scissors.
• Add decorative detail to the flowers by drawing on them with crayons.

Involving parents
Send home construction paper for parents to make FAMILY GARDENS with their children.

Sound Waves

Belonging, cooperation

○

Age **4+**

Things you will need
Nothing

Be prepared for some real silliness here. Laugh along with children. If they have a difficult time going around the circle, explain the idea of taking turns.

What to do
1. Gather the children into a circle. Tell them that you would like to see if they can make some 'copy cat' sounds, something we may call 'sound waves.' To illustrate, step forward into the circle and make a simple sound with your voice. Ask everyone to say it together. Then go around the circle, each child making the sound, one after another until everyone has had a turn. Then ask for someone to volunteer to make a different sound for everyone to copy.

2. The sequence is repeated with each volunteer: the child makes a sound, everyone says the sound together, and the sound wave goes around the circle.

Want to do more?
To make sound waves easier, ask the children to pass a ball as they make the sound. As soon as they get the ball, they should repeat the sound and pass the ball to the next person.
• With older children, start two different sound waves in opposite directions around the circle.
• Instead of a sound, try a 'body wave,' moving one part of the body: for example, arms, hands, legs, feet.

Involving parents
This would be fun for parents and children to play in the car, excluding the driver, of course.

Feet Treat

Belonging

Age 4+

Things you will need
Two plastic buckets of warm water, one soapy
Several towels
Three or four colours of tempera paint
Three or four pans for the paints
Wide paintbrushes, one for each colour
Small chair
One long sheet of white lining paper
Tape

The logistics of this activity are a little complicated. Make sure to change the water frequently. Do not pressure any child who does not wish to participate.

What to do
1. Stretch the lining paper out on the floor in the art area. Tape it down at the ends and at several points along the edges. Place a different colour of paint in each pan. Set the chair at one end of the paper.

2. Call the children to the art area. Show them the paint and lining paper. Tell them you are going to help them make a FEET TREAT to hang in the classroom. You will be the first one to show them what to do.

3. Take off your shoes and socks and sit in the chair at the head of the paper. Ask a volunteer to take a paintbrush. Choose a colour and ask the volunteer to paint the bottom of your feet. When both your feet have been painted, turn to the paper and carefully stand on it with your feet fairly close together. Sit back down and wash, rinse and dry your feet.

4. Slide the chair down slightly and ask one of the children to start. That child chooses another child to paint their feet. Help each child stand up to avoid slipping and falling.

5. The completed painting should be a row of everyone's feet. After drying, label the feet and hang the FEET TREAT along one wall in the classroom.

Want to do more?
Allow the children to walk around on the paper instead of making a row of feet.

Involving parents
Parents can use fabric paint to print a pattern using the feet of everyone in the family on a T-shirt.

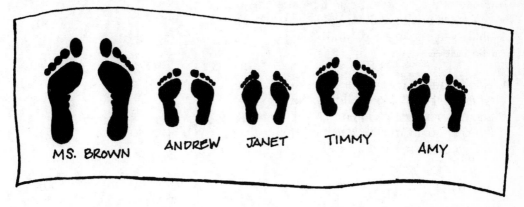

Still Water

Association, gentleness

Things you will need
Blindfold

This activity works best with small groups. With a group of more than nine, do the activity until about half the children have been blindfolded. The others can have a turn the next day.

What to do
1. Form a small circle of five to nine children. Explain the rules for the activity. Blindfold a volunteer who stands in the centre of the circle. The rest of the children hold hands and begin walking in a circle while softly chanting,
   > Around, around, around we go, and where we stop _____ *(name of blindfolded child)* won't know!

2. After a few moments, the child in the centre of the circle says, *Still water!* The circle then stops moving. The blindfolded child walks forward until they touch someone in the circle. After exploring the other child's head and clothes, the blindfolded child tries to guess that child's name.

3. That child may choose to go into the centre of the circle to begin the game again. Otherwise, call for volunteers until everyone has had a turn being blindfolded.

4. Emphasize the idea of gentleness when the blindfolded child touches another. Younger children may be unintentionally rough. Watch carefully and guide the child if necessary.

5. If the blindfolded child has difficulty identifying the child in the circle, ask the child to say a few words to provide a clue.

Want to do more?
To make the activity more difficult, ask the children to extend their hands gently toward the blindfolded person. See if the blindfolded child can guess another child's name just by touching hands.
• Or reverse roles by asking all those in the circle to close their eyes. Choose someone to go into the centre. This child can open their eyes. Ask those in the circle to join hands and walk slowly around until they hear *Still water.* The child in the centre then touches a child in the circle, who will have to guess who it is.

Involving parents
Parents can set up two kitchen chairs closely facing each other. One child sits in a chair and closes her eyes. Another family member then sits in the opposite chair. The child touches the other person's face and tries to guess their name. If only one family member besides the child is at home, wait for an extended family gathering.

My Friend

Association

○

Age **4+**

Things you will need
Music

If there is an odd number of children, join the activity yourself to create two groups of equal size. You will need at least fourteen children for this activity.

What to do
1. Divide the children into two groups of equal size. One group joins hands and stretches to make their circle as wide as possible. The second group goes to the centre and forms a second circle, facing the first.

2. When the music starts, the children in the outer circle begin to rotate in one direction while the children in the centre close their eyes. When the music stops, the children in the outer circle stop and drop their hands. The children in the inner circle open their eyes, drop their hands and run to stand in front of the person facing them in the outer circle. Each child should have only one partner.

3. As soon as partners are determined, ask each child from the inner circle to name the child facing him, quickly, one after the other.

4. When the music starts again, children who were in the outer circle go to the centre, while those who were in the centre turn to face inward, join hands and begin circling around the others.

Want to do more?
Try switching the roles of the two circles. The inner and outer circles can both face the centre and rotate in opposite directions. When the music stops, the children in the outer circle stand behind those in the inner circle. The children in the inner circle will not immediately know who is going to name them.
• Read *The Snowchild* by Debi Gliori (Frances Lincoln).

Involving parents
Parents can involve their children in a family guessing game. A parent can begin by thinking of someone in the family and giving the child a clue, for example, *I am thinking of someone who really loves spaghetti.* Keep giving clues until the child guesses correctly.

Knock, Knock

Association

○

Age **4+**

Things you will need
Two chairs

If you have more than fourteen children, you may not have time to give everyone a turn. You can play the game several times over consecutive day so that everyone has an opportunity to participate.

What to do
1. Arrange the chairs one behind the other. The front chair is 'home,' and the back chair is 'the visitor.'

2. Ask the children to sit together behind the chairs. Ask a volunteer to sit in the home chair and remain facing straight ahead, away from the other children.

3. After the volunteer is seated, point to one of the children, who will quietly take the visitor chair. After being seated, this second child should knock on the home child's chair while saying, *Knock, knock!* The child at home answers, without turning around, *Who's there?* The second child says:
   > Listen very hard, now you can't see.
   > Listen to my voice and then guess me.

4. The child at home names the visitor without turning around. The visitor then goes to the home chair, and another volunteer becomes the visitor.

5. Continue until all the children have been named.

Want to do more?
For added difficulty, have two visitors talking in unison. You could then try three or four. Can the home child name each visitor?
• Read *One Snowy Night* by Nick Butterworth (HarperCollins).

Involving parents
Repeat the family activity suggested in STILL WATER. This time, however, the blindfolded child tries to guess the other's name by listening to them talk. Encourage the family member who is talking to disguise their voice.

Hand Pictures

Conversation

Age *4+*

Things you will need
Nothing

This activity allows you to focus on the dramatic implications of movement as part of conversation. Hands can be as expressive as puppets.

What to do
1. Tell the children that their hands and fingers can tell stories or convey ideas without the use of words. Ask them, for example, to watch what your hands and fingers do and then guess which animals you are pretending to be.

2. Take your hand and arm and make a snake motion along the floor. Can they guess that your hand is a snake? Try portraying with one hand a rabbit, a bird, a spider, a fish. Can they guess each one correctly?

3. Ask the children to act out an animal with one hand. Can the other children guess the animal being portrayed?

4. Increase the difficulty by asking them to watch your hands and guess what action is happening. For example:
   You are climbing a tall tree.
   You are eating something.
   You are catching a ball.
   There are waves along a river.
   The rain is falling softly (or quickly).
   The sun has come out.

5. Ask for a volunteer to act out something for the others to identify. Encourage the children to guess. Take turns with them.

Want to do more?
To increase the difficulty, put on the following brief plays, moving your hands as though they were puppets.
   Two people are arguing, then fighting.
   Two people have decided to become friends. They approach each other and hug.
   One person feels sad, the other afraid.
   One person knocks on a door. The other answers and says 'hello'
• To decrease the difficulty, give the children answers to choose between. You might, for example, ask, *Is this a snake or a bird?*

Involving parents
Parents can play a similar game with their children at home.

gic Pocket

◯

Age **4+**

will need
Nothing

Communication means translating an idea into a form — words or gestures — that can be understood by others. Giving life to ideas through communication is critical to social life, whether we are making friends or resolving conflicts.

What to do
1. Tell the children you are going to pretend to take something out of a magic pocket. You will also pretend to use it. When you have finished you would like to see if they can guess what you took out of the pocket.

2. Take each of the following objects out of your magic pocket and engage in the suggested action.
   hammer a nail
   throw a ball
   peel a banana
   eat a sandwich
   saw wood
   cut paper with scissors
   drink from a glass
   Each time, invite the children to name the imaginary object.

3. Ask the children to take turns finding something in their magic pockets to show others in the class. Can other children guess what these objects are?

Want to do more?
Make whatever is in your magic pocket more elaborate. Take out several items with which to set a dinner table or play a game. Try unfolding objects to form much larger items like a car or a rowing boat.

Involving parents
Provide parents with instructions for playing THE MAGIC POCKET with their children.

My Family

Belonging, friendship

O

Age **4+**

Things you will need
Photographs of each child's family
Space on a notice board

Draw your own family to begin the activity. Children who cannot obtain photographs of their families will feel less left out if your picture is similar to theirs. Whenever an activity requires resources from home, plan ahead of time how to involve those children whose parents cannot or will not contribute.

What to do
1. Contact parents directly or send notes home requesting photographs of everyone in each child's family, either individual or group pictures. Children who cannot obtain photos can draw pictures of their family members.

2. Tape the pictures to a notice board or wall in clusters so that each child's family is distinct. Once all the pictures are displayed, talk to the children about family size, number of brothers and sisters, age differences and so on. *Who has a grandma living at their home? Who is an only child?* are a few of the questions you may ask. Emphasize that there are many different kinds of families.

3. Discuss the special contributions that each individual can make in their family. Try to convey the idea that children contribute to their family's well-being, for example, by giving older members an opportunity to feel proud about their ability to teach and care for someone younger.

4. Discuss the important functions of families. For example, you may ask, Why is your family important to you? What would it be like if you didn't have a family? Have you ever missed your family when you've stayed with someone else?

Want to do more?
Family portraits (see *Involving parents*) can be placed together on a notice board.
• Read *From me to you,* by Paul Rogers, illustrated by Jane Johnson (Orchard Books).

Involving parents
All the family members can draw their self-portraits on one large sheet of paper to make a single family portrait.

Missing Person

Belonging

○

Age **4+**

Things you will need
One large sheet

If the child under the sheet becomes anxious you can lightly place your hand on them to reassure them. You can also say, I'm just here. Children should not be pressurized to participate.

What to do
1. Gather the children in a circle. Briefly discuss the idea that even though people may sometimes disagree, everyone in the group is important. When someone is absent, they will be missed. Go around the circle and identify each person by name. If someone is missing from the circle, see if anyone can remember their name.

2. Tell the children that you would like them to try an activity in which someone in the group will hide. The rest of the group will try to guess who is missing.

3. Take out the bed sheet. Tell the children that you will first ask them to close (or cover) their eyes, then you will go around the inside of the circle and tap someone on the shoulder. That person should open their eyes and silently crawl under the sheet in the centre of the circle. Explain that after the volunteer gets under the sheet, you will ask the children to open their eyes and guess who the missing person is.

4. Begin the activity by crawling under the sheet yourself and allowing the children to identify you as the missing person. Then return to the circle and ask a child to take a turn. Encourage children who are self-confident and likely to feel comfortable under the sheet.

5. If no one in the group can identify them, ask the child under the sheet to say something. The children can use this clue to help them guess.

6. Make sure several children have a turn.

Want to do more?
If the group is small enough, try reversing the rules. All the children get under the sheet and close their eyes. Tap one child on the head to leave the 'tent.' The remaining children have to guess who has left. Or increase the difficulty by choosing more than one child to be under the sheet or outside the tent.
• Read *One Frog Too Many* by Mercer and Marianna Meyer (Dial, 1985).

Involving parents
Where there are three or more family members, two can hide under two different sheets. The remaining family members have to guess who is under each sheet.

Class Flag
Belonging, cooperation

✂

Age **4+**

Things you will need
Fabric paint
Paintbrushes
Sheet approximately 90 x 120 cm
(3'x 4')
Markers
Pole about 1.8 m (6') long
Stapler

Every child should be encouraged to participate. Leave space on the flag for children who are absent.

What to do
1. Stretch the sheet out on a large table in the art area.

2. Paint your school's name at the top of this 'flag.' Sketch a sun in the centre of the flag.

3. Invite the children to help you make the class flag. They can begin by filling in the sun. Draw outlines of their hands around the outer edge of the sun. One finger of each child's hand should slightly overlap with the next child's to form a circle or semicircle around the sun.

4. Write the children's names under their hands.

5. Staple the flag to the pole and hang it inside the classroom or outside the front door.

Want to do more?
Ask the group to name things that children like to do at their school. Select four activities that are among the most liked. Draw a large circle on the flag and divide it into four equal sections. Ask the children to draw one of the favourite activities in each section.
• Take the flag with you on class walks, the children taking turns being flag bearer.
• Read *Who do you Love?* by Martin Waddell, illustrated by Camilla Ashforth (Walker Books).

Involving parents
Parents and children can make a similar FAMILY FLAG at home.

Penelope's Present   ◯

Belonging, cooperation   Age **4+**

Things you will need
Nothing

In this activity, the story is accompanied by sound effects. As you tell the story, make additional comments to fill in the time as the sound effects are repeated around the circle.

What to do
1. Seat the children in a circle. Talk for a few minutes with them about taking turns. To illustrate, ask the children to say their names around the circle, one at a time, beginning with the child to your right (point). When everyone has had a turn around the circle, ask them to repeat a sound you will make with your hands. Begin rubbing your hands together. As the sound goes around the circle, ask the children to keep making that sound until you start a new sound that will also go around the circle. When the sound comes back to you, begin softly clapping your hands. The children should continue to rub their hands together until the clapping comes around to them. Do not try the rest of this activity until the children understand the idea of picking up and repeating a sound passed around their circle.

2. Once the children understand the directions, place both your hands quietly in your lap. Begin telling the story when everyone has stopped clapping. Feel free to add to or revise the story as you wish.
Once upon a time, Penelope Pig was so happy to be invited to Briarbutton the Rabbit's birthday party. She worked and worked and sewed a pretty new dress to wear. On the day of Briarbutton's birthday, she picked up Briarbutton's wrapped present (carrot stew, his favourite) and left with plenty of time because she had far to walk. Now as she walked along, the wind began to blow...(Begin rubbing your hands together.)
Oh, oh. Penelope looked up at the sky. *Looks like it might rain,* she thought. She wrapped her arms tightly around Briarbutton's present and kept on walking. (Continue with the story until the sound comes back to you. Then begin snapping your fingers on both hands.)
Oh, no! Here comes the rain. Penelope began to walk even faster now. *I don't want Briarbutton's present or my dress to get all wet,* she said. *Oh rain, please stop.* (Continue until the sound returns to you. Then begin softly clapping your hands.) But the rain fell even harder and harder and harder. Penelope's dress began to get wet...and her present to Briarbutton got soggier and soggier...when Aristotle the Mouse arrived with an umbrella and held it over Penelope so she wouldn't get so wet. (When the sound returns to you, begin snapping your fingers again.)
The hard rain stopped and changed to softly falling rain. *Looks like the rain might stop,* Aristotle said as they walked along the forest path to Briarbutton's house. (When the sound returns, begin rubbing your hands together.)
And gradually the rain began to stop and all you could hear was the wind and a few raindrops. Aristotle and Penelope finally arrived at Briarbutton's house. (When the sound returns, place your hands quietly in

your lap.)
Even the wind began slowly to calm
down...until everything was quiet.
Penelope rang the bell. *Ding-dong!*
When Briarbutton came to the door,
Penelope and Aristotle said, *HAPPY
BIRTHDAY!* Even though the box was
a bit soggy, Briarbutton loved the
carrot stew Penelope brought him.
Everyone had a great time at his party.
The End.

Want to do more?
Make up a different story from another
character's point of view.
• Invite the children to make up a story
with sounds.
• Create different sound effects with
your hands to illustrate simple stories.
• Read *Jack's Fantastic Voyage* by
Michael Foremann (Red Fox).

Involving parents
Send home a description of this activity
for parents to try with their children.
They might particularly enjoy acting out
a rainstorm at a family reunion.

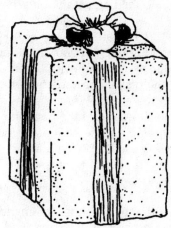

Whose Shoes?

Association

○

Age **4+**

Things you will need
Large paper bag

Consider making a few incorrect guesses to draw attention to children who are not being named.

What to do
1. Before asking the children to gather in a circle ask them to remove their shoes and bring them to you. While they are settling down, place one shoe from each pair in a large paper bag. Bring the bag with you to the group.

2. Tell the children that you are going to play a guessing game with them. Inside the bag is one shoe from each child in the group. You are going to take the shoes out of the bag, line them up and ask the children to guess who owns each shoe. Emphasize that they should not say if the shoe belongs to them.

3. Make a row of the shoes, telling the children not to start guessing until you ask them to.

4. Begin with the shoe at one end. For each shoe, ask, Now who do you think belongs to this shoe? Can you name this person in our group?

Remind the children not to say anything about their own shoes until you have gone through the entire row of shoes.

5. After the children guess the owner for each shoe, return to the first one in the row. For each shoe, say something like, *Now, some of you thought this shoe belonged to _____; some of you said it belonged to _____. Let's see who the real owner is.* Ask the child who owns the shoe to claim it.

6. When the game is finished, the children put their shoes (both of them!) back on.

Want to do more?
Children can bring toys from home in a paper bag without showing any to their classmates. Line the toys up in a row and see who can guess who brought each toy.

Involving parents
One family member sits at the kitchen table with her eyes closed. Another family member places an object in her hands. After feeling the object, she tries to guess who brought it.

Come Over

Association

Age **4+**

Things you will need
Nothing

Leaving and then joining a group that is in constant change reflects the type of informal group membership experienced by young children. Children are less likely to be overlooked if adults are present to provide guidance for both lines. Encourage children to choose someone who has not yet been named from the other line.

What to do
1. Form the children into two lines of equal length facing each other about 7.5 m (15′) apart.

2. Huddle one line together and ask someone to identify a child in the other line. Once this child is named, then begin the chant:
   Red Rover, Red Rover, let _____ come over!
   The named child leaves their group to join the group that called them.

3. The other line now has a turn to select someone to join them. The sequence is repeated until all the children have been named.

Want to do more?
To make the activity more challenging, each child can be asked to 'come over' in a different way. For example:
   Red Rover, Red Rover, let _____ skip over!
   or
   Red Rover, Red Rover, let _____ walk backwards over!

Involving parents
Parents can help their children make a telephone call to a distant family member. Letters can be substituted for calls.

Guess What Happened!   ◯

Conversation   Age **4+**

Things you will need
Nothing

Life is a drama, and a story is at the heart of every satisfying conversation. In this activity, you will use your entire body instead of just your hands to communicate dramatically.

What to do
1. Practise miming five familiar situations for children:
   Someone picking at their food, showing their dislike of it and rocking slightly as they hold their tummy.
   Someone picking flowers, smelling them and putting them into a vase.
   Someone fluffing up a pillow and falling asleep.
   Someone picking up, then feeding a baby.
   Someone taking a banana from a basket, then peeling and eating it.

2. Call the children together into a circle. Tell them you are going to act out something a person might do. When you have finished they can try to guess what you were doing.

3. Do one of the mimes and ask the children to guess the circumstances.

4. When you have acted out all five mimes invite the children to take turns miming something which the group will try to interpret.

Want to do more?
Increase the difficulty of the activity by miming more complex situations. Get up and walk around, using more space and physical action. Open doors and windows, climb ladders, play a game of catch, row a boat or perform other familiar activities.
• Explain to the children the type of activity and ask them to guess further details. For example, I'm going to pretend to eat something. See if you can guess what I'm eating. Mime eating a banana. Once the children have guessed continue with an orange, then a lollipop, then a bowl of cereal.

Involving parents
Describe the activity to parents. Suggest they introduce it as a game for the entire family. Emphasize that actions selected by adults and older children should be as simple as possible to keep a young child involved.

Name Pantomime

Association

○

Age **4+**

Things you will need
Nothing

Shy children may find it difficult to be the centre of attention. Children who hesitate or are self-conscious can perform their action while remaining in the circle.

What to do
1. Ask the children to stand, holding hands in a large circle. Tell them you have a 'name game' for them to try. Someone will start by going into the centre of the circle and saying:
   Hello there, how do you do? My name is _____ So watch what I do.
   At that point the person makes a simple motion with their body. For example, they might begin by saying the chant and then waving their arms like a bird. Then everyone responds with:
   Hello _____, We'll do it too!
   Then the entire group copies what the first person did.

2. Begin the activity by volunteering to demonstrate. Make a distinct motion with your hands, body or feet after giving your name. You can make a circle with your arms, clap your hands or turn around in place.

3. Emphasize to the children that you want them to do something that other people can copy.

Want to do more?
To make the activity more difficult, volunteers can combine movements made by two or more parts of the body -— like clapping while turning in space. Even more complicated actions, like dance steps, can be tried.
• Read *Hansel and Gretel* retold by Joyce Dunbar, illustrated by Ian Penney (Macdonald Young Books).

Involving parents
Parents can try the same activity at home, copying each other's actions.

Starry Sky

Belonging

○ ✂

Age **4+**

Things you will need
Several rolls of ribbon, each a different colour
Stars cut from construction paper, one for each person in the class
Crayons
Stapler or tape
Scissors
Display area (large notice board, wall, etc.)

Each child works separately to create something that is combined with the individual creations of others to form one single group display.

What to do
1. Write your name or draw your picture on one of the stars.

2. Bring the star and ribbons to the circle. Ask the children what they know about 'stars' and 'comets.' Discuss for a few moments.

3. Teach them the following poem:
   Stars up in the sky so bright
   Glimmer in the dark of night.
   Each of us is like a star
   Shining brightly near and far.

4. Tell the children you would like to make a display in which each of them will have their own special star. Dismiss them to the art area.

5. Give each child a star. Ask them to draw a picture of themselves on their star and decorate it as they desire. Each child can also cut two or three short lengths of ribbon to attach with tape or a staple to the bottom of the star.

6. When each child is finished, attach the stars to the bulletin board or wall. Cluster them together as a group.

7. After all the stars are attached in the display, gather the children near the notice board and discuss what they have done. Emphasize that every star is different, yet they all fill the sky together. Every star is special, just like every child in the group is special. Repeat the poem together.

Want to do more?
If you do not want to cut the stars ahead of time, draw them first on a sheet of lining paper and ask the children to fill them in.
• Read *Sophie and the Seawolf* by Jason Cockcroft, illustrated Helen Cresswell (Hodder Children's Books).

Involving parents
Send home precut stars and ribbon for parents to create a FAMILY STARS display with their children.

Family Show and Tell

Friendship   *Age* 4+

Things you will need
Nothing

Involving parents
Ask parents to provide their child with a special object from each family member to bring to school for a FAMILY SHOW AND TELL. These objects should be placed in a sturdy container. They should not be too valuable, though, in case the container is dropped. Ask them to take a few minutes to explain to their child why each person likes the objects selected.

When a child brings their container of belongings from home, make sure to label them carefully and store them safely until the child leaves for home. When other children interrupt with comments about their family, gently return the focus to the child who brought the belongings. These interruptions are acceptable as long as the child whose turn it is retains the spotlight.

What to do
1. Explain to your group that they will take turns to bring special things from home and tell the rest of the group about them, when they all gather in a circle.

2. Ask the parents of the child whose turn is approaching to gather something special from each member of their family for their child to bring to school as part of the 'family show and tell.' (See *Involving parents*.)

3. When you first gather together in a circle, ask the child to remove the objects from the container, one at a time, and tell the rest of the group who in their family likes the object and why it is special for that person. Ask the other children if someone in their family likes something similar.

Want to do more?
Family members can be asked to choose objects from a specific category, like clothes or entertainment. Pictures of the child's family can be placed on a notice board near where everyone gathers in a circle.
• Read *Grandma's Bill* by Martin Waddell (Macdonald Young Books).

The Class Gallery

Belonging

✂ ○

Age 5+

Things you will need
One long sheet of lining paper
Crayons
Tape or stapler
Display area

Making every circle the same size and shape establishes a common basis for belonging in the group. Personal decoration will emphasize individuality within the group.

What to do
1. Draw a row of identical large circles across the length of the paper, one for each teacher and child in the group.

2. Invite the children to visit the art area and draw a self-portrait in one circle. Demonstrate by drawing a portrait of yourself in a circle.

3. Write each child's name underneath their portrait.

4. The children may decorate the sheet with other drawings as long as the portraits remain clearly visible.

5. Tape the gallery to a wall or staple it to a notice board.

6. Gather in a circle near the gallery. Point out the similarities and differences among portraits. Some may have blond hair, others brown or black. Some or all the faces may be smiling. Invite the children to comment on what they see. Emphasize the uniqueness of each child in the group.

Want to do more?
The children can draw their portraits on separate sheets of construction paper instead of on one long sheet. Be sensitive to different family structures and situations.
• Also leave space at either end of the sheet for children who may join your group later in the year. Adding their portraits is an excellent way to greet and involve a new child in the group.

Involving parents
Send home a section of lining paper and a description of this activity to help parents and children make a FAMILY GALLERY.

Mystery Person
Friendship

○
Age 5+

Things you will need
Nothing

In this version of IS IT BIGGER THAN A BREAD BOX? children have to depend exclusively on verbal clues for guessing a mystery person's identity. Knowing something about each other is an important part of friendship.

What to do
1. Tell the children that you are thinking about someone in the group and that you would like them to guess who it is. You have some clues to help them guess.

2. Select yourself as the first person to be guessed. Begin with a common characteristic and gradually become more specific. The children raise their hands when they think they know who it is. For example, you might say something like, *This person likes to play with puppets ... this person likes fairy tales ... this person is a teacher ... this person is tall and has dark hair.*

3. Continue with clues about one of the children in the group.

4. After several rounds of guessing, invite one of the children to select someone and give clues.

Want to do more?
To increase the level of difficulty, give activity clues such as someone who likes to play in the sandbox, or abstract clues such as someone who has two brothers and two sisters.
• Read *Julius, The Baby of the World* by Kevin Henkes (Puffin Books).

Involving parents
Parents can try a similar activity at home, including extended family members known to their children as possible MYSTERY PERSONS.

Mystery Voices

Association

Things you will need
Tape recorder

By gradually increasing the difficulty of the activity, you will provide a challenge that keeps children involved without becoming frustrated.

What to do
1. Ask children to come individually to a quiet location where you will record their voice. Ask each child and teacher in the classroom to make the same statement, such as *I like you* or *Do you know what my name is?*

2. After everyone's voice has been taped, play the tape when you are gathered in a circle and ask the children to identify who is speaking. Play the tape at another time for children who may be reluctant to guess in a large group.

Want to do more?
Leave the tape and tape recorder at a table with a set of photos for the children to match with the voices.
• Increase the difficulty by asking the children to make a vocal sound only, like hmmmm or ohhhh. Then progress to one short word. Pause for a moment, then ask the child to make a longer statement.

Involving parents
If parents have access to a tape recorder, the entire family can play a game of MYSTERY VOICES. The children can bring the school tape home, play it for their parents and identify the voices.

Whose Hands?

Association   *Age* 5+

Things you will need
Photocopier
Pencil

Be sure to get the photocopier owner's permission before assembling children to use it. Close the cover when making the picture and clean the glass when you have finished.

What to do
1. Take the group to a photocopier and photocopy one of each child's hands. Sequence the copying in alphabetical order to help with identification. Record the names in pencil on the back of each picture. Do not let the children see the copies at this time.

2. When the children gather in a circle, show them the stack of photocopies. Tell them you are going to go through the stack, one at a time, to see if the children can guess whose hand is pictured.

3. Show each hand, one at a time, and invite the children to guess to whom it belongs. Do not tell them whether they are right or wrong. *(So you think this is Jamie's hand? Let's go through them all and then we will find out.)*

4. After completing the first round, review the set of pictures again, this time identifying whose hand is pictured.

5. At the end of the activity, pin all the hands on a bulletin board and identify them with the children's names.

Want to do more?
Polaroid pictures of hands are fast and convenient.
• You can tape a 'gallery' of hands on a classroom wall or notice board.
• Photocopied hands can also be cut out and pasted together on lining paper.
• Read *Katie's Picture Show* by James Mayhew (Orchard Books).

Involving parents
Family members can gather around a photocopier for a 'group portrait' of their hands.

What You Wear ○

Friendship   *Age* 5+

Things you will need
Nothing

This activity will give children an opportunity to do more than simply look at each other. To detect change, they will have to pay attention and look really hard at the detail that makes up another person.

What to do
1. When the children are gathered in a circle, briefly talk to them about how important everyone, each individual person, is to the group. Being noticed by others helps individuals feel comfortable in the group. Tell the children that they are going to play a WHAT YOU WEAR game.

2. Stand up and ask the children to take a good look at you. After a few moments, ask them to wait while you make a change in how you look.

3. Leave the group (or ask them to close their eyes) and make a significant change in your appearance. For example, you can take off your shoes or glasses or put on a hat. When you return, ask the children if they can spot what you have changed.

4. To make the activity more challenging, make more subtle changes, like switching your watch from one wrist to the other, untying a shoe or removing a small item of jewellery. Provide clues if the children cannot detect the change.

5. Invite the children to volunteer to be the centre of attention. Suggest what to change or add if they seem uncertain what to do.

Want to do more?
Try changing facial expressions or body postures.
• Read *Bently and Egg* by William Joyce (HarperCollins Publishers US).

Involving parents
Describe the activity for parents to try at home.

My Mobile

Friendship

✂ ○

Age 5+

Things you will need

Plastic clothes hanger for each child
Thread cut in various lengths (20–30 cm; 7"-12"); about six lengths for each child.
Several magazines with pictures of food, places, people, animals and toys
Scissors
Construction paper
Glue

This activity focuses on self-awareness as well as on sharing and learning about each other. Draw other children's attention to the mobile created by one of their classmates as the day progresses.

What to do

1. Tell the children that each of them is going to create a collection of things to hang on a clothes hanger. This arrangement is called a 'mobile.'

2. Set out the magazines and art materials. Ask the children to find a picture of food they like to eat. When they finish, ask them to find a picture of a place they like. Continue with a person, an animal and, finally, a toy.

3. Cut out squares of construction paper for each child and ask them to draw small self-portraits.

4. Glue or paste the pictures to construction paper. Make holes at the top of all the pictures and self-portraits, string a piece of thread through each of the holes. Hang each child's collection from a clothes hanger (younger children may need help).

5. Ask each child to bring their mobile when you gather in a circle. Go around the circle and ask the children to describe what they selected.

6. Hang all the mobiles in a central location. Point out differences and similarities among the children in the class.

Want to do more?

The children can simply browse through the magazines, selecting six things they like without specific categories in mind.
• Make a mobile for yourself to show children in your group.
• Read *The Minstrel and the Dragon Pup* by Rosemary Sutcliffe, illustrated by Emma Chichester Clark (Walker Books).

Involving parents

Show the parents their child's mobile. Describe the activity and suggest that each family member make their own MY MOBILE at home.

Getting to Know You   ◯

Friendship   *Age* 5+

Things you will need
Tape recorder and tape

This activity may be the most difficult for many children because it relies exclusively on verbal rather than visual information about someone else. Remember, never pressurize any children who hesitate to talk about themselves.

What to do
1. Over a period of several days or even weeks, in a quiet setting, tape an interview with each child in your group. The interview should be about five minutes in length. Ask such questions as:

    What is one of your favourite foods?
    What is one of your favourite toys?
    What is one of your special places to visit?
    Name something that gives you a sad (happy, angry or scared) feeling.

    Be sure not to mention the child's name in the interview. Once all the interviews are completed, select one to play for the group.

2. Call the children together in a circle and tell them you would like to play one interview. After the tape is played, ask the children to identify who was interviewed. Also go over the main points made in the interview. Emphasize that now the group knows more about the child than they did before. Ask the children to identify other important comments the child made.

3. Introduce the other interviews on other days, with no more than one on any particular day. Contrast — do not judge — each interview with those previously played. Emphasize that differences of opinion and feeling are acceptable.

Want to do more?
When everyone is ready for the next interview ask the children to recall information from a previous interview.
• Read *The Owl and the Pussycat* by Edward Lear, illustrated by Jan Brett (Simon and Schuster Young Books).

Involving parents
Give parents the list of questions you are asking children before making the tapes. They can help prepare their children for the activity by discussing the topics with them.

Chapter Two

Compassion

○ Circle; ✄ Art; ↔ Science; ♨ Kitchen; ❀ Open space; ✳ Outside; △ Inside

Overview

The second major goal for *The Peaceful Classroom* is compassion. Caring for oneself and others depends on remaining emotionally alive and responsive to the emotions of others. Show the children how to find words for the emotions of sorrow, anger, fear and joy. Help them to understand that feelings are different from actions and that they can express strong feelings in a positive way, and respond compassionately to the suffering of others.

As they grow up, some people insulate themselves from strong feelings, and view strong emotional experience as a form of weakness. Others may give in to the storm and allow themselves to be taken over by their emotions. They may feel powerless in the struggle to manage their passion. Some discover how to learn from their feelings and how to direct the energy of those emotions to bring them closer to others.

Use words like 'happy,' 'sad,' 'angry' and 'afraid' in any discussion with children. Children will participate in group activities like MAKE A FACE, THE LITTLE LONELY STAR and EMOTION TAGS. It is also helpful to read carefully selected picture books that focus on emotions and compassion.

Emotion Pictures

Recognition of emotions

○

Age *3+*

Things you will need

A collection of pictures cut from magazines, each showing children or adults experiencing one of the emotions listed above. Glue to identical sizes of heavy construction paper or card. Number pictures on the back. Laminate.

Some children have no words to express how they feel. They need to hear such words as 'happy,' 'sad,' 'angry' and 'afraid' if they are to understand their emotional experiences. The EMOTION PICTURES are a basic tool you will need for many of the activities in this section. With younger children, begin with basic emotions and progress to complex emotions which are more difficult to understand.

What to do

1. ACTIVITY 1: When the children are sitting in a circle, hold up one of the pictures and ask them how this person feels. (If they do not know, tell them.) Ask the children to talk about what they see that makes them think the person feels that way. Point out facial expressions or other features which suggest the emotion.

2. ACTIVITY 2: Stack at least three pictures of each emotion on a table in your classroom. Mix up the order of the pictures. Hand the stack to a child and ask him to group all the sad pictures together, then all the happy ones and so on.

3. ACTIVITY 3: Show several pictures portraying the same emotion and ask the children to identify how all the people feel.

Want to do more?

You can show illustrations from children's books that visually represent emotions.

Involving parents

Urge parents to use simple words like 'angry,' 'happy,' 'sad' and 'frightened' as they talk with their children.

How Do You Feel?

Recognition of emotions, expression

○

Age *3+*

Things you will need
A collection of pictures cut from magazines, each showing an object or situation that might trigger an emotional reaction in children. The pictures, however, should not show any obvious emotional reactions taking place. For example, your collection can include pictures of spilled ice cream, a broken tricycle or teddy bear, a spider, a dog, different amusement park rides, a skydiver, a delicious-looking dessert, a picture of a monster (for older pre-schoolers), a beautiful tree or garbage. The pictures should suggest a wide variety of emotional reactions. Glue to identical sizes of heavy construction paper or card stock.
Number pictures on the back. Laminate.

How Do You Feel? pictures are a companion tool to the EMOTION PICTURES. Instead of pictures of people experiencing emotion, the emphasis here is on situations that trigger different emotions.

What to do
1. ACTIVITY 1: When the children are sitting in a circle, hold up one picture and ask the children how they would feel to be near the object or part of the event. Emphasize that people are sometimes different in how they feel about things. Some people are frightened of spiders, for example, others are not.

2. ACTIVITY 2: Ask the children to sort through the pictures with a specific emotion in mind. For example, they could look for things that make them feel angry. Then sort them into pictures that frighten them, pictures they like and pictures that make them sad. They can choose pictures more than once.

3. Make note of which pictures the children select.

Want to do more?
For younger children, tell the group how you might have felt as a child about what is pictured.
• You can point to situations or objects illustrated in children's books.
• Read *The Velveteen Rabbit* by Marjery Williams, illustrated by William Nicholson (Little Mammoth).

Involving parents
Ask parents to find pictures of something that they felt happy, sad, frightened or angry about as a child. They can use these pictures to engage their children in a discussion about emotions.

Make a Face

Recognition of emotions, expression   ○
                                                                    Age *3+*

Things you will need
One card from the Emotions Picture File portraying each of the emotions you want to discuss.

The ability to interpret body language, especially facial expressions, is a key to understanding the emotional experiences of others. 'Reading' another person correctly is an important aspect of compassion. The face is a window to the human heart.

What to do
1. Show the children the cards, one by one, and ask if they know how each person feels. When finished, place the cards where all the children can see them.

2. Tell the children that you are going to pretend to feel like one of the people in the pictures and that you would like them to guess how you feel. Make a face that shows the emotion you chose. Repeat this several times for other pictures.

3. Continue with another round, emphasizing body language this time. For example, you might shake your fist and stomp your feet for anger. Re-emphasize that you are only pretending to have the feeling.

4. Let the children have the opportunity to demonstrate feelings by asking them to take turns choosing an emotion and making faces for the other children to interpret.

Want to do more?
With older children, choose three basic emotions. Ask for three volunteers. Whisper a different emotion to each child (or show them one of the pictures). Each child takes a turn, demonstrating the emotion through facial expression and body posture. The remaining children guess what emotion each of the three has demonstrated.

Involving parents
Parents can play a similar guessing game with their children. They can choose an emotion, make a face and ask their children to guess the emotion portrayed.

The Little Lonely Star   ◯

Problem solving, helping   Age *3+*

Things you will need
One apple for every two children
One knife

Storytelling can powerfully demonstrate how human beings affect each other emotionally. For example, a character may feel less sad after experiencing the sympathetic tenderness of another person. Understanding this cause-and-effect is a critical element in learning compassion and other forms of kindness.

What to do
1. Ask children if they know what it means to be 'lonely.' Discuss their ideas.

2. Tell them the story of THE LITTLE LONELY STAR. (Keep the apples out of sight.) Elaborate on the plot as you wish. Use simple gestures to give added drama to the story.

   Once upon a time the sky was very dark at night. There were no stars ... except one ... a very tiny star. This little star was all alone and felt very lonely all by himself in the sky. One day this lonely little star went to see a very wise, very old, old man who lived on the earth on the top of a high mountain. The lonely little star asked the old man if he could help. Because the old man loved this little star very much, and because he was very wise, he said he would do two things.

   First, the old man reached behind him and pulled out a beautiful, shiny black bag. He opened it up, reached in and pulled out a handful of shimmering, glimmering stars. With one great swoop of his hand, he filled the night sky with a thousand stars. *There,* said the wise old man. *Now you have many stars to be your friends. But because you have been so lonely, I am going to do something else for you. I am going to place you on earth, inside something special.* He snapped his fingers, and it was done. The End.

3. Ask the children, *Do you know where the wise old man put that sad little star?* (Take out the apples.) *Why, inside every apple is a place for a tiny star. Watch, and let's find out if there really is something like a star inside this apple.*

4. Cut the apple horizontally to make two equal portions. Pull the apple apart and show the 'star' to the children. Cut the other apples in half and give a portion to each child.

Want to do more?
Make up other simple stories illustrating sadness, anger and fear, each showing a compassionate reaction by one of the characters.
• Read *The Selfish Giant* by Oscar Wilde, illustrated by Katrien van der Grient (Floris Books).

Involving parents
Children can go home and tell the story and demonstrate the surprise ending to their parents. Encourage parents to look for compassionate reactions to emotions expressed in the books they read to their children.

Poor Little Sad Eyes

Expression, respect/encouragement

○

Age **3+**

Things you will need
Nothing

Children are often criticized for the way they express their emotions. Stop crying right now! a mother may insist. Don't you talk to me like that! a father demands. Criticizing how children express their feelings will not make those feelings disappear. Telling a child what not to do is inadequate. If we do not like a child's behaviour, we have to show them what to do to manage their emotions.

What to do
1. Read and act out the following poem:
    Poor little boy with sad eyes, *(point to eyes)*
    See him now, how much he cries. *(mimic crying, hands to eyes)*
    He tries to stop with all his might, *(clench teeth, grimace)*
    He doesn't know *(shake head)*
    That tears are all right. *(nod head 'yes' while pointing to 'tears')*

2. Repeat the poem, with the children joining in both the words and actions.

3. Ask the children if they think it is okay for boys and daddies to cry. How about girls and mummies? Invite them to talk about a time when they were sad.

Want to do more?
Make up your own poems about anger, fear and happiness, emphasizing behaviour that is acceptable.
• Read *Penguin Small* by Mike Inkpen (Hodder Children's Books).

Involving parents
If you have the opportunity to meet with the parents as a group, explore with them acceptable ways to express emotion, especially anger. Send home the poem for parents to read with their children. Encourage them to talk with their children about a time they cried.

Sad Teddy   ◯

Problem solving   *Age* **3+**

Things you will need
A soft, cuddly teddy bear

When we talk about strong emotions, we send children a message that these experiences are part of being human. We can also emphasize that we are able to learn ways to express these feelings that bring us together and help us understand each other. Honest tears are not a sign of weakness, but of love and strength.

What to do
1. Bring the teddy bear to school and introduce him to your children. You can ask the children to help you se- lect a name for the teddy bear. Make up a past for the bear. Tell the child- ren how he arrived at their school. Emphasize that this is a very special teddy bear who will talk about feeling sad, angry and afraid. Set very clear rules about playing with the bear (for example, no throwing, keep him in- doors, keep him in the dress up area).

2. Later in the year, use Teddy when you want to help children who are emotionally upset. For example, a child may feel sad because of the death of a pet or relative. Include Teddy when the children are gathered in a circle. Begin the discussion with something like, *Let's pretend that Teddy is very sad today. What do you think happened to Teddy?* Encourage the children to describe what they think happened to Teddy. 'Listen' to Teddy and then tell the children about what has happened. You may want to start the story yourself with a statement similar to one of the following:
   > *Teddy is sad today because he lost something very special.*
   > *Teddy is sad because a friend is moving to a different town.*
   > *Teddy is afraid today because the big boys who live near him want to hurt him.*
   > *Teddy is angry because someone broke his truck.*

3. Make Teddy's problem similar to that of the child whom you want to reach, but do not directly duplicate the circumstances. Avoid painfully harsh examples that may alarm more than enlighten. Children will benefit from this discussion by listening and offering their own thoughts, rather than by being made the centre of attention as someone with a problem.

4. Ask for ideas that might help Teddy. Ask the children to tell Teddy how they think he should respond to his

problem. Someone may want to give Teddy a hug. When you have finished, thank the children for their ideas.

Want to do more?
Do not overuse this type of activity. Introduce it when you believe a discussion about emotions would be most helpful. Balance discussions of angry, frightened and sad feelings with more positive experiences like excitement: T*eddy is so excited. He's going to stay overnight at a friend's house for the first time.* And happiness: *Teddy is so happy; his grandpa and grandma are coming to visit.*

• Read *First Flight* by David McPhail (Happy Cat Books).

Involving parents
Show Teddy to parents and encourage them to engage in similar discussions with one of the soft toys or puppets at home.

Happy/Sad Person

Recognition of emotions

○ ✂

Age **4+**

Things you will need
Cups
Grass seed
Potting soil
Felt tip pens

We often use the word 'make' when referring to the source of our emotions. We say, for example, You 'make' me so mad! 'Make' implies force and helplessness. We cannot be responsible for how we feel if we are 'made' to feel a certain way. But emotions result from how we interpret what happens to us. We speak more accurately if we say, 'I feel' angry when you say those mean things to me! By taking responsibility for our feelings, we begin to help children assume responsibility for theirs.

What to do
1. When everyone is gathered in a circle, briefly talk with the children about feeling happy and feeling sad. Emphasize that sometimes people feel happy and sometimes they feel sad. Invite them to make a Happy/Sad Person in the art area.

2. Give each child a cup. Bring out the felt tip pens and ask them to draw a happy face on one side of the cup and a sad face on the other.

3. Once the faces are drawn, help the children fill the cups with potting soil to about four-fifths of their capacity. Sprinkle grass seed in each cup and cover with a light layer of soil. Water slightly and place the cups in a row on a window sill that gets indirect sunlight. Let the children turn the cup to face whichever way they want.

4. When the grass grows, the children can cut the 'hair' into a desired shape.

5. Ask the children what they think might have happened to make Mr. Sad so sad. Ask about Mr. Happy, too.

Want to do more?
Children could also make Happy/Angry or Calm/Scared People.
• Read *Bella's Big Adventure* by Benedict Blathwayt (Red Fox).

Involving parents
Invite parents and children to make their own HAPPY/SAD PEOPLE at home.

Emotion Tags

Recognition of emotions, expression

Age **4+**

Things you will need
Five name tags, each with a drawing of a face that reflects either happiness, anger, sadness, fear or disgust. (See the illustration.) These small pictures can be laminated and hole punched at the top. Use a safety pin to wear the tag.

Sometimes we may be frightened of expressing emotions to young children. We are most vulnerable when we reveal how we feel. These moments are also opportunities for children to reach out compassionately to us. When I told Steven, a four year old in my class, that I felt sick and 'yucky,' he put his arm around me and suggested, *Now Dokker Smith, you go home and your mummy look after you.* Children who express feelings when distressed are more likely than more reserved children to help someone in trouble.

What to do
1. When you are feeling particularly happy, sad, angry or afraid, pin on the appropriate 'Emotion Tag.'

2. The tag will draw children's interest and provide opportunities to talk about the emotion you feel. Discuss your feelings if the children are interested. Use simple terms and describe issues familiar to young children. For example, *I feel sad because someone I really like does not like me anymore,* communicates clearly what you feel to young children.

3. Change tags as your feelings change through the school day.

Want to do more?
Set out EMOTION TAGS for the children to wear. The children can draw or paint their own tags.
• Read *It Isn't Easy* by Margaret Connolly, illustrated by Rosita Manahan (Oxford University Press).

Involving parents
A similar set of EMOTION TAGS can be worn by family members at home.

Emotion Drawing

Expression, cooperation

Age **4+**

Things you will need

A large sheet of lining paper
A variety of creative arts materials (glue, construction paper, crayons, paint, etc.)

Creative activity provides many opportunities for expressing our feelings. Each of us has a strong urge to communicate our emotional experiences in some way to others, if not to ourselves. This activity emphasizes expression through creative action, rather than drawing a specific picture.

What to do

1. Set out the art materials and lining paper. With your children's help, establish an emotion theme saying something like: *Okay, let's make a happy picture!* or *Let's make a sad picture.*

2. Distribute the materials and encourage the children to work cooperatively. Avoid suggesting a specific setting for the drawing, such as a circus for 'happy' drawings. Each child can contribute ideas to create a mural effect. Thank them for their cooperative effort.

3. When finished, tape the EMOTION DRAWING to a wall. Examine the picture with the children and talk about how they portrayed the same emotion in different ways.

Want to do more?

Play appropriate music while the children draw.
• They can also make drawings on separate sheets to be hung together like a gallery.
• Read *Fall Is Here! I Love It!* by Elaine W. Good, illustrated by Susie Shenk Wenger (Good Books, US).

Involving parents

Parents and children can draw together, taking one emotion as a shared theme.

How Do They Feel?

Recognition of emotions

Age *4+*

Things you will need
New pictures to add to the EMOTION PICTURES representing the basic emotions.
A large piece of construction paper to cover the pictures of emotions.
Scissors

We make assumptions about how someone else feels by observing them and finding evidence that suggests to us a certain emotion. Tears, however, can signify either happiness or sadness. Only when we combine tears with downcast eyes and a slumped body posture, are we fairly sure that the person is sad.

What to do
1. Cut a slit in the construction paper 'cover' slightly longer than the width of the new pictures.

2. In the art area, invite the children to play a guessing game with the new pictures. Keeping the pictures hidden from view, slip them under the cover. Slide a small part of one picture through the slit. Ask the children to guess how the person pictured feels. Expose slightly more of the picture and ask again. Gradually reveal the entire picture.

3. Hide a different picture under the cover and gradually expose it from the bottom up, pausing to allow the children to guess.

Want to do more?
Set out materials for the children to use with each other.
• Instead of cutting a slit, cut holes varying in size from large to small in different sheets of construction paper. Cover the emotion picture with several of these sheets, their holes overlapping, the sheet with the smallest hole should be on top. Ask the children to guess how the person feels. Remove one sheet at a time, gradually revealing more of the picture.

Involving parents
Parents can play a similar guessing game at home with their children.

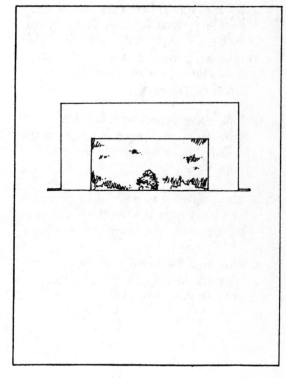

Emotion Puppets

Expression

✂

Age 4+

Things you will need
Small paper bags
Marker pens
Rubber cement
Scissors
Construction paper

Children like puppets because they can safely pretend to be someone else without fear of criticism. The ability to project oneself into another person is the basis for compassion.

What to do
1. Using a small paper bag, make a sample puppet whose face expresses one of the basic emotions.

2. Set materials on the table in the art area and invite the children to make their own happy, sad, angry or afraid puppets. Have the EMOTION PICTURES available to provide examples of facial expressions.

3. Talk about experiences you had growing up that relate to emotions the children have selected for their puppets.

4. The children can name their puppets and write the name on the bottom of the bag, with your help, if necessary.

5. Organize the furniture in the room to create a stage where children can perform their own puppet shows.

Want to do more?
Create your own puppet family, each puppet expressing a different emotion. Use these puppets to put on brief sketches for the group.

Involving parents
Children can bring home their puppets to show their parents. Parents and children can make additional puppets together.

Happy/Sad Sticks

Problem solving

✂ ○

Age *4+*

Things you will need
Two short, flat sticks (available from paint or hardware shops for mixing paint) for each child
Two small paper plates for each child
Stapler
A variety of creative arts materials (glue, construction paper, crayons, paint, etc.)

Avoid giving children the impression that there is a 'right' or 'wrong' response to the situations you describe. It may seem obvious to you what response a situation will call forth, but other people's reactions are not so predictable. How will a child feel whose toy is broken by a playmate? Angry? Sad? Or both?

What to do
1. Distribute paper plates to the children in the art area. Ask them to draw a happy face on one plate and a sad face on the other.

2. Staple each paper plate to the top of a flat stick.

3. Ask the children to bring their HAPPY/SAD STICKS you all gather in a circle. Ask them to hold up and show you the happy stick. Repeat with the sad stick. Tell them that you would like to find out how they think people feel at different times.

4. Describe each of the following circumstances. When you have finished, ask the children, How did this person feel? Happy or sad? Show me either your happy or your sad stick.

This person loves ice cream. After tea his mummy gave him some chocolate ice cream as a surprise.
This person's daddy gave them a really nice, gentle hug.
This person's favourite truck broke into lots of little pieces.
When this person came home from school, their mummy told them their dog Woofles was ill.

5. Create additional examples based on experiences familiar to your children.

Want to do more?
Make HAPPY/ANGRY and HAPPY/ AFRAID STICKS. Repeat the activity with these emotions.
• To make the activity more challenging, introduce sad/angry, angry/afraid situations. Emphasize with older children that when something happens, some people may feel sad, while others feel angry.
• Ask the children to close their eyes and imagine the situation while you talk. They can open their eyes when it is time to make a choice. This prevents your own expression from suggesting a response.
• Read *After-School Monster* by Marissa Moss (Lutt).

Involving parents
Parents and children can make their own 'Happy/Sad' Sticks at home. They can take turns describing a situation while the other chooses a response.

Contrasting Feelings

Recognition of emotions

✄

Age **4+**

Things you will need
EMOTION PICTURES
Large sheet of paper
Marker

Every emotion is a natural outcome of what we believe is true. Feeling follows thought. There are no irrational emotions, only irrational beliefs. If we believe something is dangerous, even though it is not, we will feel afraid.

What to do
1. On a large sheet of paper draw a horizontal and a vertical line to divide the sheet into four equal parts. In three sections, place pictures from the Emotion Pictures that depict the same emotion. Place a picture depicting a very different feeling in the fourth section. (see illustration).

2. Tell the children that three of the pictures go together because the people in the pictures feel the same way. One does not belong because that person feels different from the other three. Ask the children to point to the one that is different. Take the picture selected and ask, How does this person feel? After a child responds, group the three remaining pictures and ask, How do these people feel?

3. If the children cannot name the emotions, point to the group of three and say something like, *These people feel sad. Look at their faces, and see how their mouths are turned down. See the tears in their eyes. They feel sad. Now this person over here feels happy.* (Point to the fourth picture.) *See the smile on her face. She feels happy.*

4. Take note of those emotions that children cannot identify. Introduce these terms in ongoing conversations with them.

5. Repeat with other emotions. Make the session fun.

Want to do more?
Use HOW DO YOU FEEL ABOUT THIS? pictures instead of the EMOTION PICTURES. Tell them that three pictures go together because many people are frightened of these things. The other is something usually considered less frightening. Keep in mind that these situations are potentially ambiguous. There is no right answer. Ask the children to describe the reasons for their choices.

Involving parents
While reading a book or magazine together, parents can ask their children how someone in a picture feels. If the child does not know, the parent can identify the feeling.

Face Plates

Recognition of emotions

✂

Age 4+

Things you will need
Construction paper
Scissors
Small paper plates
Collage materials (wool, bits of material
and paper, etc.)
Glue or paste
Crayons or paint

Emotions like sadness, fear and anger
are often identified as 'bad' emotions.
We say, *I feel bad,* instead of *I feel sad*
(or afraid, or angry). Such a negative
evaluation is understandable given the
amount of criticism we experience for
being sad, angry or afraid. Avoid
labelling any emotion so negatively.

What to do
1. Cut out a variety of construction
   paper eyes, eyebrows, noses and
   mouths that can be combined to
   reflect different feelings. Place these
   features in the art area with the paper
   plates, glue or paste, paint and
   crayons.

2. When the children arrive, ask them to
   identify which pieces are eyes,
   eyebrows, noses and mouths. Give
   the children paper plates and ask
   them to make faces using the pieces.

3. When they are finished, encourage
   them to identify the kind of feeling
   that the face they made shows — if
   they are interested in discussing it.
   The children can then decorate the
   faces with either crayons or paint and
   the collage materials.

4. Collect all the faces and tape them to
   a wall. Encourage the children to
   identify which faces look happy, sad,
   scared — or scary — and angry.

Want to do more?
Hold up one of the plates and ask the
children to make a face that feels the
same way.
• Read *Making Faces* by Nick
Butterworth (Walker Books).

Involving parents
Parents and children can make FACE
PLATES together at home.

I'm Happy Sometimes

Problem solving, expression

○

Age 4+

Things you will need
Nothing

Happiness is the reaction we have when we believe we have been lucky or experienced something good. We want to move closer to whatever it is that is making us happy.

What to do
1. Ask the children to tell you what being 'happy' means. Tell the children a true story about a time you felt happy when you were young. Describe an experience similar to something children in your group might have gone through. What physical feelings did you have? Were you smiling, trembling, your heart pounding? What made you so happy? What did you do?

2. Let the children take turns telling the group about a time when they felt happy.

3. Teach them the following poem:
   When I'm feeling happy, *(smile)*
   The world is such a sight! *(hand over eyes 'looking')*
   Hugs for you, hugs for me, *(point to others, then hug self)*
   Smiles as bright as sunlight. *(hands outstretched)*

4. Ask the group the following questions:
   What things do children feel happy about?
   How can we help others feel happy?

Want to do more?
Older children can draw a picture or write a story about a time when they were happy.
• Read *Tattybogle* by Sandra Horn and Ken Brown (Hodder Children's Books).

Involving parents
Send the poem home for parents and children to learn together. Encourage parents to talk about some of their happy experiences growing up.

I'm Sad Sometimes

Expression, problem solving

○ Age **4+**

Things you will need
Nothing

Sadness is the emotional reaction we have when we believe we have experienced a loss. We no longer have something precious to us. A child cries after losing their teddy bear or after the death of a pet. Mourning means coming to terms with the loss and learning to live without the loved person or thing.

What to do
1. Ask the children to tell you what being 'sad' means. Tell the children a true story about a time you felt sad when you were young. Describe an experience similar to something children in your group might have gone through. What physical experience did you have? Were you nauseous, trembling, crying? Did your heart feel 'heavy?' What did you think you had lost? What did you do?

2. Let the children take turns telling the group about a time when they felt sad.

3. Teach them the following poem:
   When I'm feeling sad, *(make a sad face)*
   Sometimes I have to cry. *(run fingers down from eyes)*
   I need a hug from mum or dad *(hug self)*
   And a tender lullaby. *(grasp and rock arms)*

4. Ask the group the following questions:
   What things do children feel sad about?
   What can we do when we feel sad?

5. Talk with the children about ways to understand and manage what feels like a loss. Some suggestions include: getting adult help, talking about the sadness, finding a substitute, helping someone else, learning a new skill. Make your suggestions relevant to the losses the children describe.

Want to do more?
Older children can draw a picture or write a story about a time when they were sad.
• Read *Nothing* by Mick Inkpen (Hodder Children's Books).

Involving parents
Send the poem home for parents and children to learn together. Encourage parents to talk about sad moments they experienced growing up.

I'm Afraid Sometimes ⃝

Problem solving, expression   Age **4+**

Things you will need
Nothing

Fear is the emotional reaction we have when we believe we are threatened or endangered. Fear gives us the energy to flee or overcome the danger. See also No STRANGER TO DANGER.

What to do
1. Ask the children to tell you what being 'frightened' means. Identify several words for fear. Tell the children a true story about a time you felt frightened when you were young. Describe an experience similar to something children in your group might have gone through. What physical experience did you have? Were you nauseous, trembling? Were your hands sweaty? Was your heart pounding? What was the danger you thought was present? What did you do?

2. Let the children take turns telling the group about a time when they felt frightened.

3. Teach them the following poem:
     When I'm feeling terrified, *(make scared expression)*
     The world seems so spooky. *(look around)*
     I want to find a place to hide — *(hands over head)*
     Maybe you could help me. *(point to others)*

4. Ask the group the following questions:
     What things do children feel frightened of?
     What can we do when we feel frightened?

5. Talk with the children about ways to understand, manage and overcome what might be dangerous. Some suggestions include: getting adult help, talking about the fear, learning about the fear, avoiding the scary thing, learning a new skill. Make your suggestions relevant to the fears the children describe.

Want to do more?
Older children can draw a picture or write a story about a time when they were frightened.
• Read *The Prickly Hedgehog* by Mark Ezra, illustrated by Gavin Rowe (Magi Publications).

Involving parents
Send the poem home for parents and children to learn together. Encourage parents to talk about scary moments they experienced growing up.

I'm Angry Sometimes

Problem solving, expression

O

Age *4+*

Things you will need
Nothing

Anger is the emotional reaction we have when we believe we are faced with an obstacle that prevents us from reaching a goal. Anger provides us with the energy to overcome the frustration.

What to do
1. Ask the children to tell you what being 'angry' means. Identify several words for anger. Tell the children a true story about a time you felt angry when you were young. Describe an experience similar to something children in your group might have gone through. What physical experience did you have? Were your teeth gritted, fists clenched, hands sweaty, face hot, heart pounding, body trembling? What was the threat you thought was present? What did you do?

2. Let the children take turns telling the group about a time when they felt angry.

3. Teach them the following poem:
   When I'm feeling angry, *(make an angry face)*
   My face feels boiling hot. *(fan face)*
   I am mad, you see. *(point to self)*
   A fight? Let's not! *(fist to palm, then shake hands and head)*

4. Ask the group the following questions:
   What things do children feel angry about?
   What can we do when we feel angry?

5. Talk with the children about ways to understand, manage and overcome obstacles or frustrations. Some alternatives include: getting adult help, solving the problem, avoiding the problem, talking about the anger, learning a new skill. Make your suggestions relevant to the anger the children describe.

Want to do more?
Older children can draw a picture or write a story about a time when they were angry.
• Read *Katie Morag and the Tiresome Ted* by Mairi Hedderwick (Bodley Head).

Involving parents
Send the poem home for parents and children to learn together. Encourage parents to talk about angry moments they experienced growing up.

Emotion Dancing

Expression, cooperation   *Age* **4+**

Things you will need
Samples of music, each about two
minutes long, each conveying a
distinctly different emotional tone.
Classical music provides the broadest
range of emotion, from fear to joy. The
soundtrack to the film *Fantasia* offers
excellent examples of the type of music
you need.
One silk scarf (or substitute) for each
child.

Emotion is energy. The word derives
from the same origin as the word
'movement'. The experience of emotion
brings vitality and movement into our
lives. Fear, for example, helps us flee
from danger; sadness, to mourn a loss.
To feel is to be alive.

What to do
1. Ask the children to listen to each
   sample of music. After each sample,
   ask them how they felt while the
   music played.

2. After you have played all the music,
   give each child a scarf. Invite the
   group to stand and dance together as
   the music is replayed. Ask them to
   dance according to how they feel
   about the music.

Want to do more?
Give the children their own musical
instruments and ask them to play happy,
sad, angry and scared music.
• To introduce an element of
cooperation, ask the children to hold a
partner's hand and dance to the music
together.
• Or play music while the children
paint, and ask them to paint to the
music.
• Read *The Bear Dance* by Chris Riddell
(Little Mammoth).

Involving parents
While listening with their children,
parents can talk about how they feel
while the music plays. Parents can also
dance with their children to the music.

Feeling Face Masks

Recognition of emotions   ✂

Age *5+*

Things you will need

One large paper bag for each child
Four bags upon which are drawn either
a happy, angry, sad or frightened face
Mask materials (crayons, construction
paper, wool, paste or glue, etc.)
Scissors
Large mirror

Feelings are often confused with
behaviour. We treat some emotions with
disdain because of the associations we
make between feelings and behaviour —
anger with hitting, fear with running
away, for example. But emotions are not
'bad.' Actions may be harmful and
beliefs irrational, but emotions are a
natural part of being human. As you
respond to children's behaviour, make
statements like, I know you feel angry,
but I cannot allow you to hit Cindy. No
hitting in our school.

What to do

1. Show all the materials to the children
   when they arrive at the art area.
   Suggest that they try to make masks
   with either happy, angry, sad or
   frightened faces. Help them make
   holes at eye level so that they can
   place the bags over their heads and
   see what they look like.

2. Hand out the paper bags and
   materials and encourage the children
   to draw their own FEELING FACES.
   While the masks are being made,
   discuss various feelings, how they
   originate and their consequences.

3. Display the masks you made earlier if
   the children need help understanding
   what to do. Do not, however, use
   your masks as models for children to
   copy. Let them create their own.

4. When the children have finished,
   invite them to guess what kinds of
   feelings the others have drawn on
   their masks.

5. Under close supervision, invite the
   children to wear the masks and see
   what they look like in the mirror.

Want to do more?

Masks can also be made from large
paper plates using a rubber band stapled
to the side as a headband.

Involving parents

Parents and children can make FEELING
FACE MASKS at home together. Never
allow a child wear such a mask
unattended.

The Sound of Feelings

Recognition of emotions

Age 5+

Things you will need

Tape recorder
Cassette tape
Emotion Pictures

Deprived of all visual cues in this activity, children may have difficulty making a choice. Focusing exclusively on sound will help them observe auditory as well as visual emotional cues.

What to do

1. Convey each of the basic emotions on tape through the tone and inflection of your voice. For example, repeat a statement like *Hello, there*, giving it a different emotional inflection each time. Say it sadly, happily, angrily, fearfully. Repeat a different statement, changing the order of emotions. Repeat single words like *Yes*. Then shift to a more ambiguous vocalization like a humming sound. Make the same sound each time, but with a different emotional emphasis.

2. When everyone is gathered in a circle, place four pictures from the EMOTION PICTURES representing happiness, sadness, anger and fear in a row. Play a segment from the tape. Stop and ask the children to identify how the person saying the tape feels. Tell the children the emotion you were trying to portray. Continue with other segments.

Want to do more?

Encourage the children to make various sounds with specific emotions in mind. The teacher and the other children can try to guess what the emotion is.
• Consider placing children in back--to-back chairs to eliminate visual cues.

Involving parents

Parents can repeat the activity at home, taking turns with their children, making sounds and guessing the emotions.

Emotion Stories

Problem solving   Age **5+**

Things you will need
Paper
Crayons

The most important and dramatic moments in our lives are characterized by strong feelings. In stories, shifts in emotions are critical to plot development.

What to do

1. Decide on a sequence of basic emotions for your story. In this example, the sequence is happy-sad-happy-afraid-angry-happy.

2. Invite the children to make up a story with you. Begin with:

   Once upon a time there was a young girl just your age. One day she felt really happy about something that happened to her. What do you think happened?

3. At this point, call on one of the children to identify what the girl was happy about. Elaborate on this point in the story and move to the next emotion in your sequence. For example:
   Yes, her mummy and daddy, the queen and king, gave her a beautiful puppy for her very own. The puppy had long brown hair and droopy ears. She named him Shnooze. Together the princess and Shnooze would...(describe what they did together). Then something sad happened to the princess. What do you think happened?

4. Repeat the procedure in 3, elaborating on a child's response and moving to the next emotion in your sequence until you have finished the story.

5. Invite the children to draw pictures illustrating part of the story. Hang them on the notice board.

Want to do more?
Record the story for later listening with illustrations drawn by children.
• Choose a different sequence of emotions for another story.

Involving parents
Parents can repeat this storytelling activity at home, blending sequences of emotions into a story they create with *their children*.

Whose Feeling?

Problem solving   ○

Age **5+**

Things you will need
HOW DO **YOU** FEEL? pictures
Paper and pencil

During the later pre-school years, children begin to grow away from egocentrism — defined as the inability to understand the point of view or feelings of another person when these differ from one's own. This activity prompts children to see others as unique people with their own ideas, reactions and feelings.

What to do
1. Select one of the basic emotions. Note the choices children made for that emotion during the HOW DO **YOU** FEEL? activity. For example, for the emotion of fear Terry said the spider would frighten him, Tim said the thunderstorm and Sarah said the snake.

2. Call the children together into a circle. Invite them to play a guessing game about the things other children in the group feel afraid of (or angry, or happy or sad about). Tell them you are going to ask for a volunteer. You will show the group three pictures. One was selected earlier by the volunteer as something they find frightening.

3. Gather three pictures together: the one the volunteer chose as frightening (for example, the spider) and two that he did not (for example, the amusement park ride and the waves at the seaside). Set the three pictures in a row and say something like, *One of these three things frightens Terry; the other two do not. Which one did*

Terry select? Affirm each child's right to feel any emotion in whatever circumstance arouses it.

4. Ask for another volunteer and continue as before. Make sure to vary the order of the pictures from child to child.

Want to do more?
To make the activity easier, choose more divergent situations. In the previous example, you could combine pictures of ice cream, a pretty tree and the spider. To make the activity more difficult, choose pictures that suggest more similar circumstances, like a spider, snake and lion.
• Read *Mama, Do You Love Me?* by Barbara M. Joosse, illustrated by Barbara Lavalee (Little, Brown and Co.).

Involving parents
Parents can identify four things that frighten them, of which only one actually does. Children can guess which one really frightens their parents.

Emotion Picture Studio

Recognition of emotions, expression

○ ✂

Age 5+

Things you will need
Camera (a Polaroid is great)
Film

Keep in mind that emotions are often intermingled; they do not simply replace each other. The mother who sees her child run out into the street feels simultaneously frightened, angry and loving. At any moment, however, only one feeling will seem to predominate. Like most activities appropriate for older pre-schoolers, the success of this one builds on their experience with the preceding activities.

What to do
1. When the children are gathered in a circle, tell them you would like to take photographs of them showing different emotions. Ask them to make a sad face, then a happy face, then an angry face, then a frightened face. Invite them to come with you to your 'picture studio' near the art area.

2. The EMOTION PICTURE STUDIO is a table with a small chair at which children can sit. Children visit the studio one at a time. Ensure as much privacy as possible.

3. Ask a volunteer to sit at the table. Place one of the pictures from the EMOTION PICTURES in front of the child and ask them to make a sad (or happy, or angry, or frightened) face, too. Take a picture of the child showing the emotion.

4. When all the children have had a turn, put all the pictures together. As they did with the pictures in the EMOTION PICTURES, children can sort the photos into categories of emotion. Photos can also be used as 'flash cards' to teach children words for the basic emotions. Use only those cards that clearly show an emotion.

5. Photos can also be organized into categories of emotion and displayed on a classroom wall or notice board.

Want to do more?
Exchange photos with another class and see whether children can guess the emotions portrayed.

Involving parents
Children and parents can draw pictures of each other reacting emotionally to different situations.

Real Feelings   ○

Problem solving   Age 5+

Things you will need

Draw happy, sad, angry, calm and frightened faces on separate sheets of paper.

The idea that people sometimes act and appear one way while actually feeling another is difficult for five year olds to understand. Most pre-schoolers have not yet learned the subtle art of masking how they feel. But the rituals of emotional suppression are learned during the pre-school years. For example, in a class of four-year-olds, I once asked Stephen how he felt as he was crying. Between sobs, he told me, I feel fine.

What to do

1. Introduce the activity by saying something like, *Sometimes people do not want others to know how they really feel, so they put on a pretend face. They want to hide their feelings from others. Let's say you called me a mean name. I could smile and say, 'You shouldn't say that.'* (Pick up the happy face and then put it down.) *But even though I have a smile on my face, deep inside I feel sad because I don't like being called names. While talking, slide the sad face under the happy face.*

2. Use the following stories to illustrate your point. Keep the second picture hidden from view until the end of each story.

STORY 1: (Hide the sad face behind the happy one.) *This teacher broke a favourite dish while at home. Just after, a neighbour knocked on the door. When he answered the door, this is how the teacher looked* (show happy face). *How do you think he really felt?*
After a discussion, reveal the sad face. Explain that the teacher felt very sad because his favourite dish was broken.

STORY 2: (Hide the angry face behind the calm one.) T*here was another time when a teacher had to tell a little boy in her class that he could not do something. The little boy got into a rage and spat at the teacher. The teacher tried to remain calm. She told him he was not supposed to do that* (show calm face). *How do you think he really felt?*
After a discussion, reveal the angry face. Tell the children that the teacher was angry because she disliked being spat at.

STORY 3: (Hide the afraid face behind the angry one.) *There was another time when another teacher was outside watching children in his class play. One child climbed up on the very tall slide and began to jump up and down. The teacher saw this child almost fall off. He ran over to the slide, looked up at the child and told her to get down immediately. This is the way the teacher looked* (show the angry face). *How do you think he really felt?*

After a discussion, reveal the frightened face. Explain that the teacher was afraid because he knew that this child was in danger of being hurt.

Want to do more?
Invite the children to make up similar stories of their own.
• Read *The Dragon Who Couldn't Help Breathing Fire* by Denis Bond, illustrated by Valerie Petrone (Scholastic).

Involving parents
Parents can talk with children about times when they have not wanted to show how they were feeling.

Chapter Three
Cooperation

○ Circle; ✄ Art; ✦ Science; ♟ Kitchen; ❀ Open space; ✳ Outside; ⌂ Inside

Overview

The third major goal for *The Peaceful Classroom* programme is cooperation. The ability to work together to achieve common goals is an important personal skill. Encourage children to be aware of goals they have in common with others, to work together to achieve those goals and how to resolve conflicts without violence.

Children who have high self-esteem have a harmonious or collaborative view of personal power. They are willing to work with, not against, others. They do not have to prove their competence by dominating others through force or deception. They do not have to prove their excellence to themselves or others by winning. Their striving for improvement is based more on achieving personal or group goals than comparing themselves to others.

Instead of 'building character,' competition introduced by adults is more likely to heighten a child's fear of failure, invite comparison with others and diminish self-esteem. In contrast, cooperative activities enhance children's feelings of personal power and contribute to their sense of group belonging. Competition builds walls between people; cooperation builds bridges.

Use words like 'problem,' 'goal' and 'cooperation' in discussions with children. Children will participate in group activities like JUICY GROUP, WE'RE ALL WINNERS and BISCUIT MACHINE. It is also a good idea to read carefully selected picture books that focus on cooperation and conflict resolution.

Mouse on the Run

Cooperation

○

Age **3+**

Things you will need
One soft, small ball

Cooperation first appears in young children when they give, take and return playthings to adults. This exchange has definite rules. The child offers the adult a toy to take and then expects it to be returned immediately. Through this type of involvement, children learn how to cooperate with others.

What to do
1. Arrange the children in a fairly tight circle. Take out the ball and say something like, *Oh, look. I'm going to pretend this ball is a mouse. Hello, little mouse.* (Put your ear to the ball and pretend to listen.) *He wants to walk around our circle. He's tired, so he wants to go really slowly. So let's work together, cooperate, to pass the mouse around the circle. I will start. Okay, little mouse, here we go.*

2. Give the ball to the child on your right and ask her to pass the 'mouse' to the next person. Keep instructing the children until the mouse goes around the circle one full time without a problem. Then say, *Okay, mouse, stop! Now he wants to go a little faster. Let's see if you can make him go a little faster.*

3. Once the children understand how to take and pass the ball, you can ask them to speed up or slow down to add variety.

Want to do more?
To increase the difficulty, add another ball. Try passing it in a different direction.
• Play music of varying tempos to suggest slow or fast movement.

Involving parents
Now might be a good time to ask parents to visit to let them know about your emphasis on cooperation.

Making Dough

Cooperation   ✂

Age *3+*

Things you will need
350 g (12 oz) flour
100 g (4 oz) salt
Powdered tempera paint
100 ml (4 floz) of water
Large bowl
(Increase proportionally in order to make enough for all the children.)

Cooperation means pooling resources with others to accomplish a task. Young children are capable of cooperation. For example, nineteen-month-old toddlers have been observed taking turns while building a tower of blocks.

What to do
1. Divide all materials (flour, salt, water, tempera paint) into small portions.

2. Tell the children you would like them to make some playdough. They will have to work together and cooperate at the table to succeed. Give a small portion of one of the ingredients to each child at the table. Encourage all the children to become involved in the preparation. (For example, one child adds the water to the bowl, the next mixes in the flour, the next adds the salt, etc.) The group can pass the bowl around to take turns kneading the dough.

3. When they have finished, the group can divide the dough into portions for each child sitting at the table. Following a period of play, return the play-dough to a container designated for the group and refrigerate for later use.

Want to do more?
Other activities can be divided into tasks given to individuals within a work group. For example, prepare a salad by giving each child a specific responsibility. One child can cut or tear the lettuce, another peel the tin of kidney beans, etc.
• Read *Oliver's Fruit Salad* by Vivian French, illustrated by Alison Bartlett (Hodder Children's Books).

Involving parents
Send home the playdough recipe for parents to make with their children. Provide a small amount of powdered tempera paint, if possible.

Double the Fun (or How to Find a Partner)

Cooperation   Age *3+*

Things you will need
1 m (3′) lengths of wool, all the same colour, one length for each pair of children
Pairs of identical (in shape and colour) construction paper cut-outs, one pair for each pair of children

Many activities for children involve working in groups of two. If the children are left to pick their own partners, the ones who tend to stick together will miss opportunities to relate to different children. Here are two methods that use chance to form partnerships among children.

What to do
1. Untangling yarn: Arrange the lengths of wool side by side. Gather the ends so that they protrude about ten centimetres/four inches from your hand. Ask each child to select one end from one length of wool. When you let go, challenge the children to unravel the pieces without letting go of the end in their hand. Can they find their partner at the other end of the piece of wool?

2. Matching shapes and colours: Take each pair of construction paper shapes and shuffle them with all the other pairs. Distribute one cut-out to each child. When all are distributed, ask the children to find the one that matches theirs. This person will be their partner.

3. If there is an odd number of children, join in the activity. If not, help where needed.

Want to do more?
To make the wool activity more difficult, overlap the lengths back and forth before the children try to unravel them.
• Matching shapes can be made more difficult by reducing the number of colours and making the shapes more complex or more similar.

Involving parents
Many of the activities you suggest to parents involve children and adults working together as partners. DOUBLE THE FUN could be tried at home as a fun way to find a partner.

Juicy Group
Cooperation

Things you will need
One orange for each teacher and child
One small bowl for each child
Jug
Paper cups
Knife
Small cutting board
Spoon (to remove seeds from bowls)
Napkins
Washcloth and towels

Every child needs to feel powerful. We can help children learn to channel their personal strength to create harmony rather than disunity and conflict. Loss of power, the inability to make things happen or to make a difference — these are the roots of violence.

What to do
1. Ask the children to wash their hands thoroughly before beginning.

2. Take out your orange and hold it up for the children to see. Take a minute to talk about what they know about oranges. Cut a thin slice from the orange. Pass it around and ask the children to hold it up to the light so that they can see the beautiful design of the fibres. Can they smell the orange?

3. Pass round the bowls and napkins. Tell the children you are going to see how well they can cooperate to make a jug of fresh orange juice. Take your orange and slowly squeeze the juice into a bowl. Hold up the bowl so the children can see the juice.

4. Cut each orange into quarters. Hand a segment to each child and ask them to squeeze the juice into the bowl. When the children finish, ask them to pour their juice into the jug and begin squeezing another quarter. Comment on how each child's effort contributes to the common goal.

5. When everyone has finished, pass round the cups and pour each child some juice. Talk about how they all worked together.

Want to do more?
Use an old-fashioned glass orange juice squeezer after the children have finished squeezing to extract all possible juice from the orange quarters. Let the children eat the remaining pulp from the quarters when they have finished making juice.
• Read *Pass the Jam, Jim* by Kaye Umansky and Margaret Chamberlain (Red Fox).

Involving parents
Encourage parents and children to work together to make their own orange juice at home.

Making Butter

Cooperation

○

Age 3+

Things you will need
Whipping cream
Salt
Bread or crackers
Large jar with secure top

Although adults may have to impose turn-taking rules in group activities, young children do spontaneously take turns in the games they create on their own. This cooperation helps to establish the order and harmony that makes group play possible.

What to do
1. Pour the cream into the jar and pass it around the circle, encouraging the children to take turns looking at and smelling the contents. When the container returns to you, salt the cream lightly, cover the jar tightly and shake vigorously.

2. Pass the container around and encourage the children to shake it vigorously, too. (You may have to take several additional turns yourself.) Once the cream thickens into butter, spread it on crackers or bread and give to the children for a snack.

3. Emphasize the idea that everyone worked together and cooperated to make the butter. Discuss how it tastes.

Want to do more?
Music can be played to enhance the rhythm of shaking.
• Try the butter on different kinds of bread or crackers.
• Bring in packets of butter to compare with what the group made.
• Read *How Do I Eat It?* by Shigeo Watanabe and Yasuo Ohtomo (Red Fox).

Involving parents
Children can show their parents how to make butter at home. Family members can take turns shaking the butter jar.

We're All Winners

Cooperation

Age *3+*

Things you will need
Small area rug or other safe surface
where children can gather
Or chalk for drawing outdoors

Competition comes about when children
are taught by adults that games must
have winners and losers. No child loses
in the activities in this book. No one is
isolated or rejected because they failed.
The responsibility for reaching a goal is
shared by the group.

What to do
1. Tell the children you would like to
   see how well they can cooperate. Ask
   them to gather in a circle and lay the
   rug in the centre. Ask the children to
   pretend that it is an island. They are
   swimmers who need to reach the
   island. They will have to work together and cooperate to see how many
   of their group will fit on the island.

2. Ask the children to move to one end
   of the room. Then ask them to begin
   swimming to the island. Count the
   children as they reach the rug.
   Emphasize that no part of their bodies
   should touch the 'water' once they
   are on the island.

3. Fold the rug in half and repeat the
   activity.

4. Roll the rug into a tube and repeat the
   activity. Balance and support now
   become more important as the
   children work together to fit as many
   as possible on the available space.
   Supervise closely.

Want to do more?
Cardboard boxes can serve as boats.
Increase the surface area to make the
activity easier; decrease to make it more
difficult.
• Read *Lazy Lion* by Mwenye Hadrithi
and Adrienne Kennaway (Hodder
Children's Books).

Involving parents
Families can try to squeeze together on
rugs of different sizes or inside
cardboard boxes.

Class Nature Collage

Cooperation

✳ ○

Age 3+

Things you will need
Display board
Glue or tape
Crayons

In some families, parental pride is based on their children distinguishing themselves in comparison to others. Parents promote competition when they compare their children with other children.

What to do
1. Tell the children you would like them to work together to make a class collage of pretty things found outside. Explain what it is and is not permissible to take. Permissible objects include leaves which have fallen off trees, pebbles, things thrown away by people like bottle tops or tin foil etc. Anything that is alive or belongs to someone else should not be taken.

2. During outside play, give the children about ten minutes to find something they think is pretty or interesting.

3. Back inside, ask the children to bring what they found when they all gather in a circle. Set the display board in the centre of the circle and ask each child to place their contribution somewhere on the board. When everyone has finished, ask if they would like to change the position of their contribution.

4. When the collage is ready, glue or tape the objects to the board and display the result.

Want to do more?
Instead of gluing or taping, find a spot where the collage can be seen but not disturbed. Let the children make a freestanding arrangement to be admired over the next few days.
• With the children, look at *A Day in the Garden* illustrated by Bettina Stietencron (Floris Books). On each page encourage them to notice the differences in the garden as early morning turns to midday, to afternoon, evening and night.

Involving parents
Parents and children can make their own nature collage together at home.

Pass Round Pictures

Cooperation

Age *3+*

Things you will need

A sheet of paper and crayon for each person in the group
Tape

Terry Orlick, pioneer in cooperative games, found that, from pre-school to year two, children who experience cooperative games are three to four times more likely to continue to play cooperatively even without the presence of an adult. Children without this experience become more competitive as the years progress.

What to do

1. This activity gives children an opportunity to contribute and to receive a picture created by the entire group.

2. Give each child several crayons and a sheet of paper with their name at the top. Tell the children that they have a short time to draw whatever they want on their paper.

3. After about one minute, ask the children to pass the paper to the person on their left *(demonstrate)*. Ask the children to add to the drawing in front of them. As the pictures circulate, the children contribute to each one.

4. Stop when the drawings return to their originators. Each child now has a drawing composed of the work of everyone in the group.

5. Talk about how they all worked together to create the drawings. Tape all the pictures together on a wall.

Want to do more?

Ask smaller groups to sit around tables in the art area. Provide additional art materials (paint, glue, collage material, etc.) for the children to use in making pictures which they pass round the table.

Involving parents

Children and parents can complete PASS ROUND PICTURES at home.

Group Soup

Cooperation

○ 🍎

Age **3+**

Things you will need

Kitchen utensils and a pot for preparing and cooking soup
Food brought by children and teachers
Salt and pepper for seasoning
Soup bowls and spoons
Hot plate, if no stove is available

Terry Orlick found that children reported feeling happier when playing games based more on cooperation than competition. If given a choice, children prefer cooperation.

What to do

1. A few days before actually cooking the soup, talk with the children about the many ingredients that can go into a GROUP SOUP. Ask for volunteers to bring vegetables such as carrots, potatoes, celery, tomatoes, onions and cabbage. Just about any vegetable can be added to the list. You contribute the chicken, beef or vegetable stock.

2. Send notes home with the children requesting that the foods be brought to school on the day or day before you make the soup. Request that all food be fresh rather than canned or frozen.

3. When the children arrive on the cooking day, ask them to bring their food when you all gather in a circle. (Bring a few potatoes or carrots for children who forget their food.) Take a piece of each food and circulate it around the group. Do not allow the children to eat the food. Encourage them to get a feeling for the texture, appearance and smell of each vegetable.

4. After examining the vegetables, the children should wash their hands and go to the tables to prepare the food.

5. Supervise all food preparation. Peeling and cutting utensils can hurt. Take time to show the children how to prepare the food safely. Rinse the food after it is prepared and immediately put it into the pot. Keep any surplus amount in plastic bags for later use. Add the stock and some extra water if necessary, to the soup pot.

6. While the soup is cooking under close supervision, the children can continue with other classroom activities. Vegetable cooking times vary, so you may want to start some items before adding others. When the soup is finally cooked and served, compliment children on their cooperation in making the group soup.

Want to do more?

You can prepare some of the food and allow the children to finish. For example, cut most of the way through the carrots and let the children finish the cut with a less dangerous knife.
• Read *Stone Soup* by Tony Ross (Collins Andrio).

Involving parents

Parents can take their children shopping for vegetables, then involve them in the preparation of soup at home.

Tug of Peace

Cooperation

✳

Age *3+*

Things you will need

One rope about 2 cm (¾") to 2.5 cm (1") thick, approximately 12–15 m (40'–50') long
A very heavy, but moveable object (large wooden crate, piece of plywood holding a stack of bricks, small boulder, log, etc.)
Gloves for children (brought from home)

Never compare one child's performance with another's to motivate them to do better. Their focus should be on setting and achieving a worthy goal, instead of doing better than someone else.

What to do

1. Gather the children around you and tell them you have an activity that will require them to work together to move something heavy.

2. Tie the rope securely around the heavy object so that two equal lengths of rope remain. The object should be heavy enough that the group can only move it successfully with great effort. The rope should be strong enough to withstand the strain.

3. Divide the children into two equal groups and assign each group to one end of the rope. Ask them to put on their gloves. On command, both groups begin to pull the rope and try to move the object to a reasonable distance designated by the teacher. Supervise them closely for safety.

4. Do not hesitate to become involved. Shout words of encouragement and praise as the children pull. When finished, discuss the merits of cooperation to accomplish a difficult task. Point out that no single individual can move the object alone (let anyone who wants to, try). Only a group can do it.

Want to do more?

Have a Tug of Peace between the teacher(s) and children. Eight or nine determined pre-schoolers make a good match for a relatively strong adult. You may be surprised how strong a group of young children can be when they work together.

Involving parents

Ask parents to set up several situations in which they and their children work together to achieve a goal. For example, children and parents can lift and move a heavy box together. Parents should involve their children cooperatively even though they are capable of achieving the goal alone.

Rockabye

Cooperation, gentleness

○

Age **4+**

Things you will need
Sturdy large blanket or sheet
Music

ROCKABYE, like many activities in this book, has two distinct objectives. The children doing the rocking cooperate to offer kindness to another. The child being rocked is the recipient of both their cooperation and their kindness.

What to do
1. Stretch out the blanket and ask the group to form a circle. Talk for a few minutes about gentleness and cooperation.

2. Ask for volunteers to take a ROCKABYE ride. The volunteer lies down on their back in the centre of the blanket.

3. The rest of the group stands and lifts opposite edges of the blanket, slightly raising the child off the ground.

4. Once this is accomplished, invite the volunteer to close their eyes. Begin swinging the blanket gently back and forth. Compliment the children on their cooperation.

5. After about a minute, lower the volunteer gently to the floor and repeat with another child.

Want to do more?
Distribute adults equally around the blanket to help out with support.
• Consider playing peaceful, happy music while the child is rocked.
• Read *Hoot* by Jane Hissey (Red Fox).

Involving parents
Parents and other family members can work together to ROCKABYE one of their young children.

Biscuit Machine

Cooperation

Age **4+**

Things you will need
Small, sturdy area rug

Parents will probably find it difficult to emphasize cooperation with their children in a society that glorifies competition. Some parents may justify placing their children in competitive situations in order to prepare them for the eventual reality of winning and losing. Young children, however, first need a history of cooperation to prepare them to cope with the pressures of competition.

What to do
1. Invite the children to cooperate to make an imaginary BISCUIT MACHINE. Ask for one volunteer to be the biscuit and two volunteers to be chefs.

2. Ask the remaining children to sit in two equal lines about 1m (3') apart. They represent the ingredients. Place the rug at one end between the lines. Ask the 'biscuit' what kind of biscuit — oatmeal, raisin, chocolate etc. — they would like to be. Ask the biscuit to lie on their back on the rug.

3. When the biscuit and the chefs are ready, and each part of the machine knows what ingredient they are to contribute, then begin. For example, some children will put in the flour, some the sugar, others the raisins and chocolate. The final four children can be the oven, joining hands over the biscuit and humming as it 'bakes.'

4. Ask the chefs to pull the rug holding the biscuit between the lines to the other end, where it will be baked. Offer help if needed.

5. Repeat with another volunteer. If you have enough children, you can have two biscuits on the production line, one after the other.

Want to do more?
Make other kinds of food, too. How about a salad?

Involving parents
Families can set up their own BISCUIT MACHINES, 'salad bars' or 'car assembly lines' on a double bed or living room floor. The 'biscuit' can roll instead of being pulled from one part of the 'machine' to another.

Balloon Bounce

Cooperation

Age **4+**

Things you will need
One balloon

Children who work cooperatively are more likely to encourage others and see them as partners instead of competitors. Children who are not locked in competition are more willing to help each other.

What to do
1. Ask the children to stand and make a circle. Tell them that you have a game to play that will require working together — cooperating. You will toss a balloon into the air, and their goal is to keep it in the air without touching the ground. You will count how many times the group hits the balloon. After a child hits the balloon once, they have to go back to their place and let someone else have a turn.

2. After returning to their place in the circle, their job is to remain there and to hit the balloon back into the centre of the circle if it comes their way. Once everyone has had a turn, and the balloon has not touched the ground, the group has won. Emphasize that they should hit the balloon gently upwards into the centre of the circle to make it easier for others to hit.

3. Go to the centre of the circle and ask the children to gather around you. Then toss the balloon straight up into the air. Remind the children to go back to the circle after hitting the ball.

4. After the last child has had a turn, or the balloon touches the ground, begin again and encourage the group to improve on its previous score.

Want to do more?
Lay a rope along the floor to provide a boundary. Divide the children into two groups and ask the groups to move to opposite sides of the rope. Ask the groups to bounce the balloon back and forth across the boundary without letting it strike the ground. Count the number of hits the children make. When the balloon strikes the ground, start again and encourage them to beat their previous score.
• Read *The Runaway Train* by Benedict Blathwayt (Red Fox).

Involving parents
Parents and children can repeat the activity at home.

Puzzles for Us

Cooperation

○ Age **4+**

Things you will need
Different colours of construction paper
Scissors
Envelopes

Children who experience the value of
cooperation are more likely to work
cooperatively in the future.

What to do
1. Make simple puzzles by cutting sheets
   of construction paper into three
   different pieces (see the illustration).
   Place each set in an envelope.

2. Divide the children into groups of
   three. When they are ready, tell them
   you have a puzzle for them to solve.
   Each child will get one or more
   pieces, and together they will have to
   solve the puzzle.

3. Give each group an envelope. Tell
   them that each envelope has puzzle
   pieces in it that together form a
   rectangle. Ask each child to take a
   piece of the puzzle from the
   envelope. When everyone has a
   piece, ask them to put their puzzle
   together. Encourage their efforts and
   give hints where necessary.

4. When a group completes a puzzle,
   give them a more difficult one to do.

5. When you have finished the activity,
   talk about how well they worked
   together and cooperated, to solve the
   puzzle problems.

Want to do more?
Make the activity more difficult by
increasing the number of pieces and
making each piece less distinctive (see
the illustration).
• Make the task easier by cutting the
sheets into two pieces and asking the
children to form partnerships instead of
groups of three.
• Let the children make puzzles for
others to solve.
• Read *What If*, by A.H. Benjamin,
illustrated by Jane Chapman (Magi
Publications).

Involving parents
Parents can purchase or make simple
puzzles appropriate to their child's age
and assemble them together.

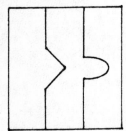 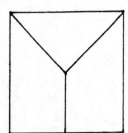 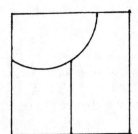 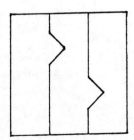

Balloon Pick-Up

Cooperation

○

Age **4+**

Things you will need
About 25 balloons
Kitchen timer

Increased competition distracts children from experiencing the pleasure of accomplishment. They become more preoccupied with the performance of others.

What to do
1. Blow up all the balloons and put them where they will not drift around the room (e.g., in a corner behind some chairs).

2. Divide the children into groups of three. Reconvene in a circle and ask the groups of three to sit next to each other.

3. Tell the group that you would like to see how well they can cooperate. Each group of three will try to get as many balloons as they can off the ground before the timer buzzes. One child will be the 'balloon stuffer' while the other two hold balloons be-tween their heads, hands, tummies, legs, etc. The balloon stuffer becomes a balloon holder after the other two are holding as many balloons as they can.

4. Set the timer for about two to three minutes. Begin the timer and count each balloon held off the ground. Cheer the threesome on. When time runs out, or they have held as many as they can, another group will take a turn.

5. If the children become preoccupied with each threesome's score you could encourage them to count an overall total, to which each threesome's score contributes.

Want to do more?
For added challenge, blindfold the two holders. Now the stuffer has to give more direction to the holders.
• Decrease or increase the time to change the difficulty level.
• Read *The Blue Balloon* by Mick Inkpen (Hodder Children's Books).

Involving parents
Parents and children can do the activity together at home.

Back Stand

Cooperation

Age **4+**

Things you will need
Nothing

A competitive environment increases tension and frustration and can trigger aggressive behaviour among the winners as well as the losers.

What to do
1. Ask the children to form partnerships. Tell them that you would like to see how well they can cooperate. Ask partners to sit back-to-back. When they are ready, ask them to stretch out and interlock their arms with their partner's. You will probably have to demonstrate this.

2. When their arms are interlocked, ask them to work together to stand without letting go of their partner's arms.

3. When the children are finished, ask them to sit facing each other with their legs slightly bent and their feet touching. They should then take hold of each other's hands. Can they pull each other up to a standing position?

4. Encourage the children in their efforts. Comment on their attempts to cooperate.

Want to do more?
Try getting three or four children to sit back-to-back and stand with their arms interlocked. Ask these larger groups to sit facing each other with each child taking the hands of two others in the group, and lifting each other to a standing position.

Involving parents
Parents and children can try passing an egg to each other from one teaspoon to another.

Basket Catch-It

Cooperation

❁

Age **4+**

Things you will need
One small basket for each child
One beanbag for every two children

Set up conditions you believe to be challenging but not too frustrating. Allow children to change the rules to adjust the game to the most enjoyable level of difficulty. Inflexible rules are the hallmark of competitive games. Such rules place more skilled children at an advantage.

What to do
1. Tell the children you would like to give them an opportunity to work together and cooperate. Ask them to choose partners.

2. When everyone has a partner, form two lines with partners facing each other. Give each child a basket. Hand the beanbags to the children in one line. Tell the partners they will have to work together to throw the beanbag and catch it in the baskets. They can set their basket on the ground when it is their turn to throw.

3. After five to ten minutes of throwing and catching, ask the children to come together in a circle. Talk with them about how well they worked together.

Want to do more?
Change the difficulty of the game by increasing or decreasing the size of the basket or the distance between partners.
• Read *Eric the Reindeer* by Alison Bartlett (Hodder Children's Books).

Involving parents
Parents can try BASKET CATCH-IT at home.

Body Drawing

Helping, cooperation

✂

Age **4+**

Things you will need
Sheets of lining paper about a child's
height in length
Crayons
Paint
Collage material
Glue
Chalk (if outside)

Competition undermines generosity.
People focused on winning are not likely
to give to their competitors. Cooperation
strengthens generosity because
achievement becomes a shared goal.

What to do
1. Ask the children to choose a partner.
   Give each pair a sheet of lining paper.
   Set the art material on a nearby table.

2. Tell the children they will have to
   cooperate to complete this art activity.
   They are going to help each other
   draw pictures of their bodies. Ask
   them to decide who will go first.

3. The volunteer lies down on the sheet
   of paper. The partner draws around
   the contour of the volunteer's body to
   create an outline.

4. When the outline is finished, both
   children work together to add detail
   where desired with the art material.
   Tape the completed drawings on a
   classroom wall to form a class gallery.

5. Give the pair another sheet of lining
   paper and repeat the activity with the
   other partner.

Want to do more?
Work in teams of three instead of two.
• Make a class gallery using different
colours of chalk on a safe pavement or
on the playground if possible.

Involving parents
Send home long sheets of lining paper
for parents and children to use working
together to make BODY DRAWINGS.

Stick Together

Cooperation, gentleness

Age **4+**

Things you will need
Record turntable or tape player
Lively music

Children in our culture learn that winning requires conflict. Someone has to lose. In most cases, there is only one winner. Under these conditions, even winning becomes uncomfortable and unsatisfying. With cooperation, everyone can achieve.

What to do
1. Divide the children into groups of two.

2. Ask the children to pretend that their bodies are really sticky. What would happen if different parts of their bodies actually stuck together? What would that be like?

3. Begin playing the music. Say *Okay, let's see your hands stick to your partner's hands. What about your toes? Do they stick together?* (Follow with knees, ankles, elbows, etc.) After a few commands, ask them to switch partners. Encourage the children to be gentle in their contact.

4. After several rounds, sit down to relax and discuss how well everyone cooperated.

Want to do more?
Ask partners to maintain contact while moving around, if possible.
• Ask partners to join with other partners to make a group of four.
• Read *Any Room for Me?* by Loek Koopmans (Floris Books).

Involving parents
Parents and children can play STICK TOGETHER at home.

Two Islands

Cooperation, negotiation

Age **4+**

Things you will need
Two medium-sized area rugs
Two 25 x 150 mm (1" x 6") boards
about 1.5 m (5') long

Under no circumstances should the
boards be raised more than a few
inches. Owing to the increased risk of
falling, closely supervise any activity
requiring balance.

What to do
1. Tell children the following story:

   Once upon a time there were two
   islands. One island had a lot of trees
   and pretty rivers; the other had
   beautiful mountains and rich green
   valleys. After a while, though, the
   people living on these islands became
   tired of seeing only what was around
   them. They wanted to see the pretty
   things on the other island. But there
   was no bridge, and it was too far to
   swim. How could they solve their
   problem?

2. Place the two rugs about three
   metres/nine feet apart. Divide the
   children equally between both
   islands. Once everyone is on an
   island, set a board down on each
   island.

3. Tell the children you would like to
   see if everyone from one island can
   get to the other without falling into
   the 'water.' Anyone who touches the
   'water' will have to return to their
   island to start again.

4. Encourage the children as they
   proceed. There may be more ways to
   solve the problem than the obvious.

Want to do more?
Give the children a rope and see
whether that suggests additional
strategies.
• For an interesting challenge (a good
place to start with five year olds), create
three islands, a far island about three
metres/nine feet away from a middle
island, and a near island about five
metres/fourteen feet away. Each gets a
two metre/five foot length of board. The
goal is to get children on the near and
far islands to switch places.
• Add more islands of different
distances, each with a different length of
board.
• Read *Mr Bear to the Rescue* by Debi
Gliori (Orchard Books).

Involving parents
Parents and children can try TWO
ISLANDS at home, using rolled up rugs for
logs if boards are not available.

Bubbles in a Basket

Cooperation

❀

Age 4+

Things you will need
Bubble solution and blower
2 m (6') length of rope
Small lightweight container (like a plastic bowl)
Timer

Encouragement is sometimes difficult to distinguish from pressure. What we thought was encouragement could turn out to have been pressure, if we react to a child's failure with disappointment or hostility.

What to do
1. Divide children into groups of four. Tell them you would like to see how well each group can cooperate. Each group will have a turn trying to blow a bubble across the room so that one of the partners can catch it in a basket.

2. Lay the rope across the floor in a line to form a boundary at one end of the room. Choose one team to go first. One child takes the container and goes behind the boundary. Position the other three partners at the opposite end of the room.

3. Set the timer for about two to three minutes. Blow a few bubbles well up in the air near the group. Encourage them to work together to blow one of these bubbles across the room to their waiting partner before the timer goes off.

4. If the bubble breaks, then make another one for them at that spot.

5. When the timer goes off, give the next group in line a turn.

Want to do more?
Place the rope in a circle. The catcher cannot leave the circle.
• You may increase or decrease the size of the container to make the activity easier or more difficult.
• Increase the number of children in a group to make it easier.
• Give the children a piece of construction paper to use as a fan if they get tired of blowing.

Involving parents
Parents and children can cooperate with a game of *Bubbles in a Basket* at home.

Cat and Bird

Cooperation

○

Age **4+**

Things you will need
Three balls, two of the same colour, one of another colour

This game has an extra element of complexity as two goals, escape and capture, are simultaneously pursued by the group.

What to do
1. Arrange the children in a fairly tight circle. Take out the ball that does not match the others and say something like, *Pretend this ball is a bird. Hello, little bird.* (Put your ear to the ball and pretend to listen.) *She wants to walk around our circle. She's tired so she wants to walk very slowly. So let's work together, cooperate, to pass the bird around the circle. I will start. Okay, little bird, here we go.*

2. Give the ball to the child on your right and ask her to pass the 'bird' to the next person. Keep instructing the children until the bird goes around the circle one full time without a problem. Then say, *Okay, bird, stop! Now she wants to fly across the circle. Whenever I say 'stop and fly', stop the bird and roll it across the circle to someone else. Let's try that now. Okay, bird, walk around the circle.* Make the bird stop, fly and then walk several times so the children understand how to move the bird around and across the circle.

3. Stop the bird and hold up one of the two balls of the same colour. Say, *Oh, no! Here's a cat. I will start the cat around the circle, too. If the cat catches the bird, what happens? Remember, the cat can only walk*

around the circle. You can walk the bird around the circle or make it fly by rolling it to someone else. Let's see if the cat can catch the bird. Add the cat to the circle when the bird is directly opposite you. Stop the action and explain the rules if children become confused.

Want to do more?
Once children become adept at managing two characters, add another 'cat' to make it easier to catch the bird.. A second cat will increase the frantic action to chase and escape.
• Read *The Hare and the Tortoise* retold by Caroline Castle (Piccolo Picture Classics).

Involving parents
Parents and children can play a game of CAT AND BIRD at home. If there are fewer than six people, enlist the help of friends and neighbours and their children.

Cooperative Towers   ❀

Cooperation, negotiation   *Age* **4+**

Things you will need
Several small wooden blocks, of various irregular sizes

Our educational system is based on competition. Children are often pitted against each other in competing to be the first with the 'right' answer. One child's failure to answer 'correctly' becomes another's opportunity to succeed.

What to do
1. Invite the children to try a difficult cooperative game. Demonstrate by asking one child to be your partner. Begin by placing one block in the centre of the table. Ask your partner to choose a block and place it on top of the one you have just played.

2. If they succeed, it is your turn again. You have to place a third block on the tower, either upon the first or second block.

3. Turns pass back and forth with each person attempting to balance an additional block on the tower.

4. Players can place blocks anywhere on the tower that they wish, as long as the first block played is the only block to touch the table. Once the tower collapses, the game is over. Count the number of blocks balanced and suggest trying to improve the score the next time.

Want to do more?
Limit the number of blocks to about twenty. Be sure to include several cylindrical pieces of various widths and lengths to increase the challenge.

• You can increase the number of children in a group from two to four or five.
• This activity can be made easier by increasing the size of the blocks and cutting them to a uniform shape. The more slender the block rod, the more difficult the task.
• Read *The Long Weekend* by Troon Harrison and Michael Foreman (Red Fox).

Involving parents
Parents and children can play a game of COOPERATIVE TOWERS using scrap blocks of wood or a combination of cans and food boxes stacked on the kitchen floor.

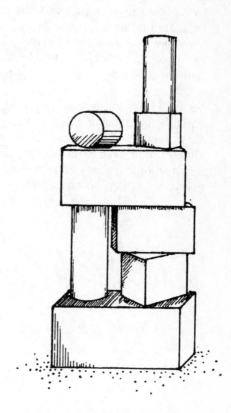

Chair Jam

❀

Cooperation

Things you will need
One chair for every child
Record turntable or tape player
Music

Few things are more painful than being
dropped out of a group for failing. Many
of us can remember the embarrassment
of losing in a spelling test or leaving the
group in a game of musical chairs.
Failure becomes associated with
rejection.

What to do
1. Tell the children they are going to
   play a game of MUSICAL CHAIRS with
   different rules. Instead of dropping out
   of the game, everyone will stay.
   When the music stops, everyone must
   be seated either in a chair or in
   someone's lap. Instead of competing
   to sit one in each chair, the children
   will have to cooperate to sit together.

2. Set the chairs in back-to-back lines of
   equal length. Start the music. When it
   stops, take away one chair. The
   children will have to share a gradually
   diminishing number of chairs until
   everyone is piled up on one chair.

Want to do more?
Ask the children to form twosomes or
threesomes to walk around the chairs.
Ask these smaller groups to stay together
throughout the game.

Involving parents
Parents can play a variation of this game
using fewer chairs and singing a song
instead of playing a record.

Telephone Friends

✂

Cooperation, friendship

Age **4+**

Things you will need
One medium-sized empty tin can for each child
Screwdriver
Tape
A 5 m (15') length of string for every pair of children
Construction paper cut to fit around the cans
Glue
Crayons

Parents may unwittingly foster competition not only by comparing, but by reinforcing their children's achievements rather than the effort they make. For some parents, trying hard is not enough. Only success earns their love.

What to do
1. Punch a tiny hole in the centre of one end of the cans with the screwdriver. Remove the other end. Cover any sharp edges with tape.

2. Ask the children to find a partner and visit the art area where they can work together, cooperate, to make telephones.

3. Set out the crayons and construction paper. Give each pair two sheets of construction paper. Ask them to sit close together and work on a decoration for their telephones. When they have finished, help them to glue their drawings to the cans.

4. Insert the ends of the string through the holes in the two cans. Make large knots so that neither end of the string can be removed.

5. Demonstrate how to stretch the string to talk and listen. Give them the phones and encourage them to have conversations in different places either inside or outside on the playground.

Want to do more?
Increase the length of the string to make the activity more challenging.
• Or make two sets of telephones for each pair of children, so they can talk and listen at the same time. This requires much more coordination between them.

Involving parents
Partners can take turns bringing their telephones home to use with their parents.

Hot Potato Stories   ◯

Cooperation   Age **4+**

Things you will need
Nothing

In order to succeed with HOT POTATO
STORIES, children have to link their
comments to those that precede them.
They have to take turns and listen
patiently until they have an opportunity
to contribute.

What to do
1. Tell the children you have a
   cooperative game to play in which
   they will work together to make up
   their own special story. Tell them you
   will begin. After you tell the story for
   a short while, you will stop, and
   someone else will continue the story.
   Then another child will have a turn.
   After that child tells some of the story,
   someone else will keep it going, and
   so on until all the children have
   contributed to the story.

2. Once you are sure these instructions
   are understood, begin with the
   following 'story stem' (or make up
   your own). Elaborate as you proceed,
   providing detail to make the story
   more interesting.

   Once upon a time, a little girl and a
   little boy lived next door to each
   other and were friends. They were
   tired of being bossed around by all
   the adults. One day they decided to

run away, so they gathered food into
two little bags. When no one was
watching, they left along a road near
their homes.
Pretty soon the road went right into a
forest. 'This is strange,' they thought,
'We didn't know there was a forest
near our homes.' Well, they didn't
want to go back, so on they went,
right into that forest. At first, the air
was warm, the sun sparkled down
through the leaves, and they could
hear beautiful bird sounds. But then
the forest turned dark and cold, and
scary sounds came from all around.
The children decided to leave the
forest. When they turned to go back,
though, the path was gone, replaced
by big rocks and thorn bushes. With
every step they took, the path
disappeared behind them, for this was
a magic path. Well, they had nowhere
to go but straight ahead.
After a little bit, there was a bend in
the path. They heard something
coming from around that bend,
something they could not see. But
they could hear it coming. The two
children stopped and hugged each
other tightly. Then suddenly from
around the bend came a....
At this point, invite children to keep
the story going. No one should
interrupt the new teller until they stop.
You can repeat and ask simple
questions to help the new speaker

elaborate. *(Oh, no! It was a dragon! What colour was it? Was it a nice or a nasty dragon? What happened next?)*

3. When you think the children are ready to end the story, pick up the story line with a prepared ending. For example:
Suddenly, the little girl became very tired and lay down on the forest path. She immediately fell asleep. She awoke to someone shaking her arm. 'No, no, get away,' she thought. Then she opened her eyes. She was in her room, and her mother was shaking her arm. 'Time to wake up and go to school, Sarah.' 'Oh, Mummy. I had the (funniest, scariest, most exciting) dream! It was about (briefly describe).' 'Wow, what an exciting dream,' her mother said. 'It was!' replied Sarah. The End.

Want to do more?

Invite storytellers to your class to tell short stories to the children. Perhaps they can finish with a HOT POTATO STORY of their own. Use simpler stories and take less time when telling stories to younger children.

Involving parents

Children can teach their parents how to do HOT POTATO STORIES at home.

Crossing the Bridge

Cooperation, negotiation, helping

Age **4+**

Things you will need

Two 2.5 m (8') lengths of 25 x 150 mm
(1" x 6") boards (Each board should be
equal in length to a line of half your
children standing side by side.)

Margaret Mead describes several non-
competitive cultures in her books. The
Zunis and Iroquois for example, both
emphasize the basic principle of
cooperative rather than individualistic
behaviour. Her research shows that
competition is culturally conditioned,
not an innate human characteristic.

What to do

1. Tell the children that you have a
   difficult problem for them to solve.
   Lay the boards flat, end to end, in a
   straight line. Ask half the group to line
   up on each board. Once everyone is
   on a board, say, Let's pretend you are
   on a bridge. Let's see if everyone on
   one part of the bridge can get to the
   other side of the bridge. Help each

other as much as you can. Do not
step off the bridge until everyone has
changed sides.

2. In the second round, lay the boards
   parallel to each other and about
   60 cm (2') apart. Challenge the
   children to cross from one bridge to
   the other.

Want to do more?

With older children, raise each bridge
about 8 cm (3") off the ground using
building blocks. This increases the
drama of the activity.
• Increase the width of the boards to
make the activity easier.
• Read *Welcome Home Little Bear* by
Maurice Jones, illustrated by Anna
Currey (Oxford University Press).

Involving parents

Parents and children can play CROSSING
THE BRIDGE at home, using boards or
rolled rugs.

Rope Runners   ✤

Cooperation, consideration for others, negotiation   Age **4+**

Things you will need
One 1 m (3') length of rope, knotted at
both ends, for each pair of children

The simple act of movement is made
much more complicated when linked
with another person. ROPE RUNNERS
requires constant awareness of and
adjustment to another person. Partners
must work together to be successful.

What to do
1. Ask the children to form partnerships
   and give each pair a rope. Ask each
   child to hold onto one end of the
   rope. Tell the children you would like
   to see how well they can cooperate
   with their partners.

2. Ask the partners to walk from one
   point to another without letting go of
   the rope. Then ask them to run
   together.

3. Set up a safe obstacle course for them
   to climb over and under, maintaining
   a grip on the rope at all times.

4. See whether they can stay together as
   they work towards other goals. Ask
   them, for example, to build a tower of
   large blocks or to eat together during
   playtime or lunch.

5. Ask two partners to play simple
   games together like tag or catch.

Want to do more?
To increase the challenge, blindfold one
of the children (supervise closely).
• Play a game of cooperative musical
chairs with partners (see Chair Jam).
• Read *Sports Day* by Nick Butterworth
and Mick Inkpen (Hodder Children's
Books).

Involving parents
Parents and children can play ROPE
RUNNERS together at home.

Cooperative Drawing

Cooperation, consideration of others

○ ✄

Age **4+**

Things you will need
Crêpe bandages, enough for each pair of children
Crayons
Large sheets of paper

An activity like COOPERATIVE DRAWING can frustrate children who have not had prior experience with cooperation. To enjoy this activity, they must have learned the patience to cooperate. Children who find this one too difficult should be introduced to simpler cooperative activities like those in the beginning of this chapter.

What to do
1. Talk with the children for a few moments when they are gathered in a circle about cooperation. What is cooperation? Can they describe examples of cooperation? Tell them you have a cooperative activity for the art area. Ask the children to find a partner. Explain how many partners can work at the same time — one set for each ace bandage. Determine the order in which children will participate.

2. Ask the partners to sit close to each other at the table. Spread the paper between them and set out the crayons. Tell them that you would like to see if they can draw a picture with their arms tied together.

3. Wrap the bandage gently but firmly around the right wrist and lower arm of one child and the left wrist and lower arm of the other. Place crayons of different colours in their hands and ask them to begin.

4. Emphasize the rule that only the hands tied together can draw the picture.

5. If children are willing, you may repeat the process, switching hands.

Want to do more?
Partners can try finger painting instead of drawing.
• Place a sponge between their wrists to increase comfort.
• For additional challenge, blindfold one child, if they are willing, and place a crayon in their hand. The other partner is neither blindfolded nor given a crayon. After a drawing is made, switch sides.
• Read *Punch and his Friends* by Coby Hol (Floris Books).

Involving parents
Parents and children can try COOPERATIVE DRAWING together, passing the drawing back and forth.

Pick Up With Sticks

Cooperation

Age **4+**

Things you will need
Two slender lengths of wood, about 600 mm (24") long by 25 x 50 mm (1" x 2").
A balloon, football, tennis ball, golf ball or similar substitutes
A container no higher than 2.5 cm (1") to hold the balls (a large cardboard box, cut to about 15 cm (6") in height would work)

Sometimes pairing children of a similar developmental level will be less frustrating for them than the results of random assignments or letting children choose their own partners.

What to do
1. Set the balloon and the container next to each other in the centre of the circle. Tell the children you would like to see if they can cooperate with a partner to put the balloon into the container. When one child volunteers to try, select a partner for them.

2. Give each child one of the wood sticks. Tell them the object of the game is for them to work together, to cooperate, to pick up the balloon with their sticks and place it into the container. Encourage the rest of the group to cheer them on.

3. If they succeed with the balloon, continue with the football, then the tennis ball and, finally, the golf ball. If the balloon is too difficult, take turns being each child's partner, coaching them as you proceed. Step back and let them try as partners once again. Be generous with your words of encouragement as they work together.

4. When they have finished, give others an opportunity to try as well.

Want to do more?
Vary the size, shape and firmness of the objects to be picked up.
• Vary the lengths and shape of the sticks. Long poles, such as broom handles, are the most difficult to handle. Make the task difficult enough to provide a challenge, but not so difficult as to be unnecessarily frustrating.

Involving parents
Parents and children can work together on a similar task at home. Suggest a simple activity like picking up a small crumpled piece of paper with two butter knives. For a more exciting challenge, try picking up a boiled egg.

Carry Boards

Cooperation, consideration for others, negotiation

Age **4+**

Things you will need
Two 1 m (4') lengths of a 20 x 120 mm (1" x 5") board
Objects that can be placed on the boards with various degrees of stability
2 m (6') length of rope

Competitive societies tend to rush children toward adulthood. They are less likely to trust children to set their own pace toward success and work independently together outside of adult control.

What to do
1. Divide the children into pairs. Line up the partners at one end of the room. Set the rope down as a boundary at the other end of the room.

2. Give the first set of partners a board and ask them to hold the board parallel to the ground. Set a fairly stable object on the board. Tell the children you would like to see if they can cooperate to carry the object on their board across the boundary without letting it fall off.

3. While they are moving, comment on their ability to watch and adjust to their partner's actions. Encourage and praise their efforts.

4. When the first pair are about halfway across, repeat with the second pair in line.

Want to do more?
You can time the children as they move across the room and encourage them to move faster the next time they try.

• Make the activity more difficult by creating obstacles the children have to move around and over.
• Make it even more difficult by blindfolding one of the partners (supervise closely).
• Read *Little Red Train to the Rescue* by Benedict Blathwayt (Red Fox).

Involving parents
Parents and children can do a similar activity at home using any long, narrow object in place of a board.

Over the River

Cooperation, consideration for others, negotiation

Age **4+**

Things you will need
40 cm (15″) strip of cloth
Sponge
One 2.5 m (8′) length of a 25 x 150 mm
(1″ x 6″) board
Two small area rugs

As children learn to share power voluntarily through cooperation, natural leadership talents begin to emerge. In a competitive society, adults prefer to remain in control. This can result in power games instead of children just spending time together and creating their own games.

What to do
1. Divide the children into pairs. Tell them you would like to see how well they cooperate.

2. Lay the board down, bridging the two rugs, and say *Let's pretend this board is a bridge between two islands. The water is very deep. Let's see if you and your partner can cooperate to cross the bridge from one island to the other.*

3. Ask the children to line up behind one of the islands. Tie the ankles of the first pair together, using a sponge to cushion their ankles if needed. Tell the children to work together to cross the bridge to the other island.

4. If they fall off, invite them to return to the end of the line to try again. If they fall off a second time, let them step back onto the board and continue.

5. Continue until all the children have had a turn.

Want to do more?
Change the difficulty level by increasing or decreasing the length of the board.
• Try tying the children's hands together at the wrist.
• Or invite three children to cross the bridge together.
• Ask children to hold hands as they cross. If they break hands, they will have to begin again.
• Read *We're going on a Bear Hunt* retold by Michael Rosa, illustrated by Helen Oxenbury (Walker Books).

Involving parents
Parents and children can play OVER THE RIVER at home, substituting a rolled rug for the boards, if necessary.

Roller Ball

Cooperation

Things you will need
A piece of thick posterboard approximately 900 x 500 mm (36" x 24")
A marble or very small ball
Cup

As in all cooperative games, the less direction the teacher gives, the more effective the activity. Demonstrate, encourage — and step away. Show children what to do, then cheer them on, giving further directions only if necessary. Step away from the leadership role if you can. Remain as a participant in the game.

What to do
1. Invite the children to find a partner and try a cooperative game. Demonstrate the game to explain the rules.

2. For this game, position the board at a sloping angle on top of a table so that the lower end of the board meets the very edge of the table. One child will position and roll the marble from the top of the slope to a partner holding a cup to catch it as it rolls off the end of the board.

3. Hand the marble to one child and the cup to the other, saying *Start by rolling the marble from the top of the board. Let's see if your partner can catch it before it hits the floor.*

4. Start with a gentle slope. Increase speed and difficulty by increasing the angle of the slope.

5. Encourage children to take turns rolling and catching.

Want to do more?
Increase the size of the ball and/or the cup to make the task easier.
• Try adding different textures to the slope's surface. Glue a few small pieces of wood to the surface to create barriers that affect the roll of the marble.

Involving parents
Parents can play a similar game at home with a piece of cardboard, a marble and a cup.

Class Garden

✳ ✂

Cooperation, caretaking

Age *4+*

Things you will need
Seeds
Garden tools
Small green trees cut from green
construction paper, one for each child
Notice board
Marker

The CLASS GARDEN should be a shared,
group effort. Instead of one child
digging, planting, watering and weeding
one plant, each child should have some
responsibility for a large area if not the
entire garden. For example, one child
can water the garden, three can be
responsible for removing weeds, etc.

What to do
1. Just before planting time arrives,
   gather in a circle near the spot where
   your garden will be. Talk about seeds
   and growth. How does the earth
   nurture a seed so it grows? What do
   plants need to survive when they
   appear? Talk about what it means to
   be a caretaker or steward of the
   environment.

2. Discuss garden plans with the group.
   Where will the garden be? What kinds
   of plants will it contain? Use plants
   that mature early in the growing
   season. Show them the pictures on
   the seed packets. Make a list of all the
   tasks required on the notice board.
   This will become the assignment
   board.

3. Go to the art area and help the
   children decorate and write their
   names on the small green tree shapes.

4. Ask the children to come together in
   a circle with their trees. Consult the
   notice board. Go over the
   responsibilities involved in beginning
   the garden. Engage the children in
   deciding what they will do. Tape each
   child's tree next to their task on the
   board.

5. Change responsibilities and make
   adjustments on the notice board as
   your garden progresses.

Want to do more?
When the garden begins to mature, take
Polaroid pictures to give the children.

Involving parents
Encourage parents to start a small family
garden or indoor potted plant
arrangement. Family members can share
responsibilities for the plants.

Not Enough

Negotiation

○

Age 4+

Things you will need
About three or four objects the children will want to have

In this activity, something is offered to the group which cannot easily be divided among its members. The situation produces a conflict that the group then seeks to resolve. Enterprising four year olds in one of my groups solved the problem of being given four balloons by suggesting that I went to the shop to buy more (they all thought that was a good idea, but did not want to wait); that I did not give them away at all (most disagreed with this idea); that I cut them in half (a few pointed out that this would not work); and, finally, that I gave out four now and brought more to give out the next day. The group decided that this last suggestion was the best. Through a gradual process of negotiation, the children selected four in their group to receive the four balloons.

What to do
1. Tell the children that you have something to give them, but before you can proceed there is a problem they must solve. Set out the objects and say something like, I would like to give you these, but I think we may have a problem. What do you think it is? After the children identify the problem — not enough to go around — ask for their help finding a solution.

2. Engage the children in discussing how the objects should be given out. Do not impose your solution. Try to persuade the children to discover some mutually agreeable solution of their own. See that everyone's ideas are discussed. Encourage the children to make their own decisions. Point out the consequences of suggested choices. For example, ask What would happen if we cut them in half?

3. If the group cannot find an acceptable solution, you may suggest alternatives for them to discuss.

Want to do more?
Decrease the size of the group to make the problem solving easier.
• *Read The Doorbell Rang* by Pat Hutchins (Bodley Head).

Involving parents
Parents can also introduce simple conflicts for their children to negotiate. There is only one piece of pie left. What shall we do? Or You both want to play with this truck. How can we solve this problem?

Won or Two

Negotiation, generosity   ○

Age **4+**

Things you will need
A napkin per pair of children
One nutritious biscuit (or other food) for each child

Children may respond to this activity in several ways: the recipient may promptly consume the biscuit; the biscuit may be accepted and divided and a portion returned to the original giver; the biscuit may be given only after considerable negotiation. Many possibilities exist when the second biscuit is then placed on the napkin. Children who divide the first biscuit are likely to repeat that 'equity' strategy. Most of the children who give without receiving in the first round are likely to wait to receive the second biscuit from their partner. In some cases, children will give both biscuits to their partners without hesitation.

What to do
1. Ask the children to wash their hands thoroughly. When they are ready to join you in a circle tell them you have biscuits to give them, but that they have to find a partner and solve a problem first. Once everyone has a partner, ask them to sit facing each other around the circle.

2. Place the napkins between the pairs of children. Put one biscuit on one partner's napkin. Ask the children not to touch the biscuit yet. Explain, Here is the problem. The rule is that you can only get the biscuit if your partner gives it to you. You cannot take it for yourself. Remind the children of this guideline if they forget.

3. Ask them to begin. Remind them that they cannot take the biscuit for themselves. When all the biscuits have been given away, put out a second biscuit for each pair.

4. Ask the children how they solved the problem. Emphasize the cooperation that took place.

5. If someone has been left without a biscuit, consider giving one to them and thanking them for their generosity

Want to do more?
Use small inexpensive trinkets and other giveaways instead of biscuits. Begin with two different food items placed on the napkin.
• Read *Full Moon Soup* by Alastaire Graham (Bennett (David) Books Ltd).

Involving parents
Emphasize to parents the importance of getting children to think about conflict rather than simply following through with adult suggestions. They can encourage children to become confident problem solvers. Engage them in brainstorming many possible solutions to a conflict. Once this pool of ideas is created, then begin choosing a solution.

Jet Plane

Cooperation, helping, gentleness

Age *4+*

Things you will need
Nothing

You will need at least seven children for this activity. Supervise them closely. Be one of the lifters only if you have to do so for safety's sake. You may have trouble cooperating with the children on this task because of the size difference. Also, if you become too involved, children may look to you for guidance rather than working together as a group.

What to do

1. Involve the children in a brief discussion about aeroplanes and flying. After a few moments, ask if one of them would like to pretend to be a jet. Other children in the group will cooperate to help the jet fly.

2. Ask the volunteer to lie down on their stomach and spread their arms straight out to the side to form wings. Ask the other children to get on their hands and knees and crowd around both sides of the volunteer. When they are in position, ask them to slide their arms under their chest and legs.

3. When everyone is ready, ask the lifters to stand slowly at the same time and raise the jet off the ground. Once everyone is standing, ask the lifters to fly the jet slowly across the room. After a brief flight, ask them to land the jet slowly.

4. While the jet is flying, tell the lifters something like You are doing a great job cooperating together. Great!

5. Repeat with other volunteers.

Want to do more?
If your group is big enough, you can have two jets flying at the same time. A small area rug can serve as a landing strip. The jets can take off and land on the 'runway.'

Involving parents
Explain the activity so that parents and older children and other friends or relatives can take younger ones for a flight.

Rocket

Helping, cooperation

Age **5+**

Things you will need
A small, sturdy, child-sized chair

Cooperative games depend on trust. Everyone is expected to contribute to the extent of their ability. Individuals in the group rely on each other to do their share.

What to do
1. Set the chair in the centre of the circle. Talk with children for a few moments about rockets. Has anyone flown in a plane?

2. Tell the children you would like to pretend the chair is actually a rocket. Ask if someone would like to take a ride in the rocket. The volunteer sits in the chair.

3. The remaining children crowd around the chair, finding the best available handhold. Count down from ten. On 'blast-off,' everyone slowly lifts the chair. Supervise carefully and help when needed. With the rocket ship elevated, go for a short cruise around the room. Return to the launch pad.

4. Repeat with other volunteers.

Want to do more?
Use a small rug to provide rides on a magic carpet.
• Read *On Top of the World* by John Prater (Bodley Head).

Involving parents
Parents can take their children for ROCKET rides at home on a sturdy chair. Adult friends or older children should try only if a parent is available.

Rubber Band

Cooperation

Age *5+*

Things you will need

A rope equivalent in length to a line of all your children standing side by side

Research shows that, over time, children gradually begin to prefer easy tasks to challenging ones. Fear of failure erodes the adventurous spirit prevalent in young children.

What to do

1. Tie the ends of the rope together.

2. Place the rope on the floor in a circle. Ask all the children to grab the rope and pick it up together. Ask them to face the centre of the circle and take one step after another, backwards, until the rope is stretched as far as it will go.

3. Tell the children you would like to see how well they can cooperate. You would like them to move in the same direction, keeping the rope stretched as much as possible. Ask the group to move towards a nearby object.

4. Remind them that everyone has to work together to keep the rope stretched.

5. If the group moves success-fully, ask them to cover more distance. Ask them to walk faster and then slower.

Want to do more?

For an added challenge, call the game Rubber Band Leader. Ask one child to go to the centre and be the leader. The rest of the group has to keep the circle stretched around the leader as they walk. Can they keep the leader in the centre?

• When you yell *Switch!* everyone drops the rope, runs to the centre, then returns to a new spot in the circle.

• To add to the challenge, ask everyone to go inside the circle, raise the rope behind them and take steps backwards until the rope is totally stretched. Ask them to let go of the rope with their hands. See if they can maintain the tension in the rope so that it will remain off the ground as they move as a group from one point to another.

Involving parents

Parents and children can try RUBBER BAND at home, involving friends and relatives if needed to make a large enough group.

Mule Team

○ ✿

Cooperation

Age *5+*

Things you will need
2 m (6') length of rope

Like many games in this book, MULE TEAM should emphasize cooperative effort rather than successfully crossing the boundary. The boundary is there as a goal for the group. What counts is that they work together. Emphasize effort, not achievement.

What to do
1. Begin with the following story:

   Once upon a time there was a miner who worked in a gold mine. He worked and worked and worked until he found lots of gold. He was so excited because he had finally found the treasure he had hoped was there. He gathered it all up in a bag and got ready to go to the bank in town. But the gold was too heavy for him to carry. Oh, no! Now what was he to do? He couldn't carry it by himself. One of his friends stopped by and gave him a mule. But the bag was still too heavy. Then another friend stopped by and gave him another mule. But still the bag was too heavy. Then another friend brought a third mule. Now he had enough help. If they cooperated, all worked together, the miner and the mules could carry the gold to the bank. The End.

2. Invite the children to pretend to solve the miner's problem. Ask for three volunteers to pretend to be mules, one to be the miner and another to be the sack of gold.

3. Lay the rope down at one end of the room. If the children cross the rope, they have reached the bank.

4. Bring the volunteers to the opposite side of the room. Have the three 'mules' to get down on their hands and knees, close together and facing the same direction. Help the 'bag of gold' lie on his stomach across the backs of the mules. The miner should remain near the mules, helping to keep the gold on their backs. When everybody is ready, cheer them on to reach the bank.

Want to do more?
Set up an obstacle course of pillows or rolled blankets or rugs for the MULE TEAM to cross on the way to the goal. Supervise closely.

Involving parents
Two adults or older children can work together to provide a MULE TEAM ride for younger children.

Copy Cat

Cooperation, consideration of others, conversation   *Age* 5+

Things you will need
Three chairs

The activities in this and other chapters build on one another. Five-year-olds who have little experience with this type of activity may find one like COPY CAT frustrating. If they do, regardless of their age, start with the simpler activities found earlier in each chapter and work your way to the more difficult.

What to do
1. Set chair number one down in the centre of the circle. Set chair number two directly behind chair number one, facing in the same direction. Place chair number three so it faces chair number one. Shift chair number two slightly to the side so it has a clear view of chair number three.

2. Tell the children you have a 'copy cat' game for them to try. Ask for three volunteers to sit in the chairs. Give instructions when the children are ready.

3. Whisper in the ear of the child sitting in chair number two to hold one hand up in the air. Ask number three to act like a mirror and copy whatever number two does. Ask number one to act like a mirror and copy whatever number three does. At this point, number one and number two should be making the identical gesture. Go to the next step if they have understood so far.

4. Invite the child in chair number two to perform very slow movements with their arms and hands. See if all three can work together to create a similar motion.

5. After a few minutes, let the threesome change positions. When each has had a turn, let another group of three try.

Want to do more?
Instead of making arm or hand gestures, number two can try facial expressions.
• For greater challenge, remove the chairs and ask number two to make any type of slow motion movement in place.

Involving parents
Encourage parents to play a simple mirror game with their children. One person slowly makes a face or a motion while the other copies. Roles can be reversed to provide opportunities to be both a leader and a follower.

Card Partners

Cooperation, consideration for others, conversation

✂

Age 5+

Things you will need

Several four-card sets, two cards with identical faces and two with different ones (see the illustration).
A barrier between partners that will allow them to see each other's faces but not their hands (e.g. a felt board sandwiched between blocks).

Making the pictures fairly similar will challenge children to find the right words to help their partners choose correctly.

What to do

1. Set the barrier up on a table.

2. Ask the children to find a partner with whom to play this game. They will have to work together to solve a problem. One child will be a 'teller' and the other a 'guesser.'

3. The partners sit on opposite sides of the barrier. Give the 'teller' one picture and the 'guesser' a complete set of cards.

4. Ask the teller to describe their card to the guesser. The guesser then chooses one card from their own set, shows it to the teller and asks Is this it?

5. If the guesser is incorrect, ask the teller to describe the picture a little more. Give the teller hints for making a more thorough description. If the guesser's choice is correct, ask the partners to switch roles and continue with another set of cards.

Want to do more?

Make the activity more challenging by using more abstract drawings and increasing the number of different cards given to the guesser.

Involving parents

Make several sets of cards and directions for children to take home. The children can teach their parents how to play at home.

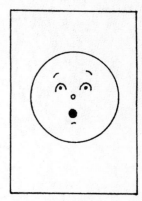

Joint Goal

Cooperation, consideration for others, negotiation

Age *5+*

Things you will need
Medium-sized box
Large, soft ball
36 cm (14") strip of cloth
Timer
Sponge

As children move through school, their self-confidence is gradually eroded as their achievements become more exclusively associated with winning. There is only room for one person at the top.

What to do
1. Ask the children to find a partner. Tell them you would like to see how well they cooperate to kick a ball into a goal. They will have to work together because one leg will be tied to their partner's.

2. Set the box on its side at one end of the room. Ask the partners to line up at the opposite end. Place the right leg of one partner and the left leg of the other close together and tie securely, but not too tightly, at the ankle with the strip of cloth with the sponge between their ankles as a cushion.

3. Set the ball in front of the two children and tell them the object of the game is to kick the ball with their tied legs into the box on the other side of the room before the timer goes off.

4. Set the timer for about three minutes and ask the children to begin.

5. When the timer goes off or they reach the goal, repeat with the second pair in the line.

Want to do more?
To change the level of difficulty, increase or decrease the size of the box and/or the ball.
• Try getting two pairs of children to kick two balls into the same box. When one pair is successful, they can go help the other.
• For a real challenge, tell the children to kick the ball backwards.

Involving parents
Parents and children can play JOINT GOAL at home.

Drop in the Bucket

Cooperation

Age 5+

Things you will need
Small soft ball
Large container such as a cardboard box or bucket
Blindfold

Comparison is a natural part of growing up and evaluating one's abilities. Such evaluation need not be competitive. Each person should be able to reach a goal and help others along the way. One person's success need not depend on another person's failure. The success of one can inspire the other to succeed.

What to do
1. In this activity, the blindfolded child is guided by a partner to drop a ball into a container.

2. ROUND 1: The blindfolded partner takes the ball and turns several times in place. He then holds the ball out for the other partner to catch in the container.

3. ROUND 2: Set the container next to or behind the blindfolded child. Invite the other child to direct the blindfolded child to drop the ball into the container. Let them exchange roles and repeat as desired. If they are proficient at this activity, they may move to Round 3.

4. ROUND 3: After one partner is blind-folded, place the container several feet away and put the ball into the container. Now the goal is for the other child to direct the blindfolded child to the container to remove the ball. Repeat as desired. Once Round 3 is completed, invite them to try Round 4.

5. ROUND 4: Give the blindfolded child the ball and place the container several feet away. The partner then guides the blindfolded child across the room to drop the ball into the container.

6. Remain close to the blindfolded child to ensure safety.

Want to do more?
With older children, you can place stationary obstacles like chairs or even other children in the mover's path to increase the difficulty. Supervision becomes even more important when such obstacles are used. As in Night Flying in the Kindness chapter, you may have to help the partners understand simple directions for movement.
• Read *The Wonderful Adventures of Nils* by Selma Lagerlöf, illustrated by Lars Klinting (Floris Books).

Involving parents
Parents and children can play DROP IN THE BUCKET at home.

Peace Table

○ ✄

Negotiation, problem solving

Age *5+*

Things you will need
Large piece of felt or a woollen blanket, at least 1 x 2.5 m (3' x 5')
Decorative materials (bits of felt and cloth, glitter, tiny stars, etc.)
Markers
White glue

The PEACE TABLE creates a setting that provides a retreat from conflict so that discussion and problem solving can take place. The presence of the PEACE TABLE is a clear signal to stop hitting, yelling or crying and start talking.

What to do
1. Ask the children for examples of disagreements. Describe a few of your own. How do people feel when they disagree? What can happen when there is an argument?

2. Spread the felt blanket out in the centre of your circle. Tell the children that this blanket is the group's PEACE TABLE. When there is a disagreement, those involved can have a 'sit down' around the PEACE TABLE to talk and find a way to solve the problem.

3. Teach the group the following poem:
   Come to the Peace Table,
   talk and be free.
   What you want, and I want,
   We can talk to agree.

4. Take a small toy and lay it in the centre of the blanket. Say something like, *Let's pretend _____ (name a child) and _____ (name a child) both want to play with this _____ toy. They will sit on opposite sides of the table. I will sit on another side of the table to help them talk to solve their problem. Neither one can take the toy until a solution is found. Does anyone have any ideas how a disagreement about who gets to play with the toy could be solved?* Ask the children for their ideas.

5. After a few moments of discussion, go to the art area to decorate the PEACE TABLE. Write each child's name somewhere on the PEACE TABLE.

6. In the future, when there is a disagreement, bring out the PEACE TABLE as a way to prompt discussion and problem solving. Use the felt blanket only for this purpose.

Want to do more?
Once the children become accustomed to solving problems with the PEACE TABLE, you may find them using it without your help. Your assistance as a mediator will be valuable, but independent problem solving, without your help, is the ideal.
• The PEACE TABLE will calm children down and help to focus conversation on seeking agreement. It is a symbol of non-violence.
• Read *The Bungle in the Jungle* by Paul Geraghty and John Bush (Red Fox).

Involving parents
Parents and children can make their own PEACE TABLE at home to use when disagreements arise.

Chapter Four

Kindness

○ Circle; ✄ Art; ❖ Science; 🍳 Kitchen; ❀ Open space; ✳ Outside; ⌂ Inside

Overview

The focus on friendship, compassion and cooperation has provided a foundation for the development of kindness, the fourth and last major goal of *The Peaceful Classroom* programme. The ability to offer, accept and ask for kindness is a critical part of social relationships. The person who cannot be kind is isolated, if not rejected by others throughout life.

The Peaceful Classroom programme views kindness as a combination of several complementary skills: taking care, gentleness, helping, generosity, sharing, protection and encouragement. Try to nurture each of these skills in children.

Young children are naturally 'egocentric.' This does not mean that they are selfish. Young children's kindness is always offered from their own point of view instead of understanding the other person's needs. A toddler, for example, may try to comfort his sick mother while she sleeps by giving her his teddy bear. The teddy bear comforts him so he believes that it will do the same for his mother. As children grow older, they are better able to offer more effective help from the perspective of the person who needs it.

Use words like 'care,' 'gentle,' 'generous' and 'protect' in our discussions with children. Children will participate in group activities like OUCH, LOTION MOTION and POOR LITTLE SAD EYES. It is also to read carefully selected picture books that focus on kindness.

Growing Flowers

Looking after plants, gentleness

○ Age *3+*

Things you will need
Flowering potted plant

Understanding the needs of living things is a prerequisite for looking after them. Gentleness is based on respect and appreciation. A simple activity involving the care of a plant is a good way to begin.

What to do
1. Show the plant to children. Talk about what the plant needs to grow. Emphasize the importance of being gentle when touching the flower. What would happen if someone grabbed or slapped it? Invite the children to touch and smell the flower gently, one at a time.

2. Talk to the children about how a flower grows from a tiny seed. Begin with the planting of the seed, then describe watering, sprouting and stem and leaf growth.

3. Act out the following fingerplay with the children:
   Tiny seed planted just right.
   Not a breath of air, nor a ray of light. *(Cover right fist with left hand)*
   Rain falls slowly to and fro,
   And now the seed begins to grow.
   (Remove left hand and slowly uncurl right fist)
   Slowly reaching for the light
   With all its energy, all its might.
   (Right hand makes creeping motion upwards with fingers together)
   The little seed's work is almost done,
   To grow up tall and face the sun.
   (Stretch out fingers of right hand)

Want to do more?
With older children, pass the plant around the circle. Emphasize being gentle.
• Ask the children to bring a potted plant from home to show the group.
• Compare two plants with different needs for sun and water, for example, a cactus and a primula or pansy.

Involving parents
Encourage parents to give their children the responsibility of caring for a potted plant at home. They should make sure their children understand what to do to care properly for the plant.

Plant Life

Looking after plants, gentleness

Things you will need
Enough seeds for all the children (use dill, chive, marigold or other seeds that germinate quickly)
A container filled with soil for each child
Marker

In this activity children are given the responsibility of planting a seed and caring for the plant that sprouts over a period of time. They will need to be reminded every day of their responsibility to care for the growing plant. Consider posting a list of duties with all their names that they can tick off after completing tasks.

What to do
1. Take the seeds out of the package and show them to the children. Talk about seeds and discuss how they grow when put into soil and watered.

2. Place the containers on the table. Ask the children to plant their seeds. Label the containers with the children's names and place them in a sunny spot.

3. Water and care for the plants. A tick chart listing necessary care and the children's names is helpful.

4. Talk with the children about the care that seeds need to help them grow. Extend the discussion to the care babies and young children need to grow to healthy adulthood.

Want to do more?
Let children take the plants home after they begin to germinate and grow.
• Ask the children to keep their plants with them for a period of time. If they take them outside, for example, they should find a safe place for the plants while they play.
• Depending on the season, children can replant their plant outside in a small school garden. Responsibility for watering and weeding can be divided among the children.

Involving parents
Encourage parents and children to grow their own herb garden of chives on the window sill.

Adopt a Tree

Looking after plants, cooperation

✳

Age **3+**

Things you will need
Fertilizer
Buckets for water
Simple gardening tools

This activity asks children to become involved with life outside their classroom, life over which they have little control. They begin here to expand the radius of their responsibility.

What to do
1. Tell the children that they are going to find a little tree outside for the class to 'adopt.' This means that everyone will have some responsibility for keeping the tree healthy so that it will grow up big and strong.

2. Take the children outside and look for the youngest tree within easy walking distance of your school.

3. Sit around the tree and discuss what it needs to be healthy. What kind of care does the tree need from the children? How will this care change over the rest of the school year? Identify the specific actions the children will do to look after the tree: pulling weeds, trimming grass, fertilizing, providing water from buckets, mulching around the base of the trunk and checking for harmful insects.

4. During the next week, assign responsibilities for looking after the tree and form a plan for continued care for the rest of the year.

5. Revisit the tree occasionally to check its progress.

Want to do more?
Invite a horticulturist to visit your group to talk about looking after trees.
• Conduct a field trip to a lawn and garden centre.
• Read *A Mother for Choco* by Keiko Kasza (Simon and Schuster Young Books).

Involving parents
Parents and children might be able to visit a local park or an area of common land, and ADOPT A YOUNG TREE growing in an unmaintained area. They can take care of the tree during periodic visits though it may be necessary to check with the local residents or park keepers that this acceptable. A picnic near the tree might be nice at certain times of the year.

Gentle People

Gentleness

○

Age 3+

Things you will need

A small, tame pet like a guinea pig or hamster

Pets provide wonderful opportunities for children to learn to be gentle and to look after a living thing. Since a pet's sudden movements may startle a child or lead to rough handling, stay with the pet when you let a child hold it. Be particularly cautious with children who have a history of aggression. Even the most active child can be very gentle when it comes to handling animals. Be aware that deliberately rough treatment of an animal is usually preceded by silly behaviour.

What to do

1. Ask the children if they understand what gentleness means. Discuss various ways people can be gentle with each other. Tell the group that you would like to give them the opportunity to be gentle.

2. Bring the pet into the circle and explain that you would like to see how gentle they can be. Giving assistance where needed, pass the animal around the circle. Bypass children who do not want to handle the animal and gently take it away from those who are too rough. Clearly identify any inappropriate behaviour and suggest more suitable responses. Comment on any gentle behaviour you see, saying something like, *Well done, Matthew, you're being really gentle with the guinea pig. You are being very careful and kind.*

Want to do more?

The same activity can be done with an egg if you are worried about using an animal.
• Read *The Shepherd Boy* by Kim Lewis (Walker Books).

Involving parents

Parents can take their children to a neighbour's or relative's house to meet and hold a pet. Or they can visit the pet shop to hold various animals.

I Cannot See

Helping, consideration for others

○
Age **3+**

Things you will need
One blindfold
Three objects that make a sound or can be touched or smelled

This activity introduces blindfolds to children. Children will have the opportunity to see how a blindfold works without having to wear one themselves. They will also have a simple opportunity to help another person. You should have an assistant in the room with you to supervise the children while you wear the blindfold.

What to do
1. Talk with the children about 'blindness.' Have they ever met someone who is blind? How do blind people learn about the world around them? Discuss why other senses like touch, sound and smell are important for blind people. Show the objects you have selected and discuss how a blind person could experience each one.

2. Tell the children that you would like to pretend to be a blind person. During the time you are wearing the blindfold, you would like them to find things in the classroom to bring to you to touch, smell or hear.

3. Put on the blindfold and ask the children to make their selections. As the children bring objects to you, take a few moments to touch, smell and listen to them by shaking or tapping them. When you have finished, give them back to the children to return to their original place.

4. After exploring each object, remove the blindfold and gather the children around you to thank them for their help. Summarize what you experienced.

Want to do more?
For an added challenge, ask one child to take you to a specific location in the classroom.
• You can introduce this activity on three consecutive days, asking first only for things to smell, then things to hear and, finally, to touch.
• Try the activity outside if there are other adults to supervise the children.
• Read *Berlioz the Bear* by Jan Brett (Puffin Books).

Involving parents
Parents can close their eyes at home or outside, and children can bring them things to touch, smell and hear.

Nature Tribute

Looking after our world, gentleness, generosity, respect

○ ✳

Age **3+**

Things you will need
Natural things in your area

Learning to respect nature begins during the pre-school years. Nursery children are Animistic in their thinking — they view all the life around them as having consciousness and motivation. They are quite happy to respond to a tree or bush as though it has feelings.

What to do
1. Discuss the idea that people can be kind to nature as well as to people. Give examples of such kindness: keeping a picnic area clean, leaving wild flowers unpicked so others can appreciate them, or providing fertilizer and water to a tree or plant. Tell the children you have an activity that allows them to be kind to nature.

2. Draw attention to a nearby object of nature, such as a tree, large rock or plant. (See also ADOPT A TREE.) Each group member looks for an interesting object found in nature — leaves, twigs, pebbles, moss or feathers — to decorate the object. Ask the children to sit around or close to the object and encourage them to discuss what they like about it. Invite them to touch the object gently and place their decoration on or near it. Ask them to chant the following poem with you:
    Hello little/big _____, (tree, plant, rock, bush)
    We really like you.
    Thank you for living
    Where we can enjoy you.

3. You can also sing a song or play a game as you sit around the object.

Want to do more?
Search the area around the object for litter. What belongs and what does not belong in nature? Collect and remove the rubbish.
• With four-year-olds and older, read *Brother Eagle, Sister Sky: A Message from Chief Seattle* by Chief Seattle, illustrated by Susan Jeffers, (Puffin Books).

Involving parents
Teach the poem to parents. The family can gather around something near their home.

Bird Dinner

Looking after our world

Age **3+**

Things you will need
Pine cones or apples
Lard or peanut butter
Dry cereal hoops
Bird seed
String
Scissors
Box

In their efforts to care for wildlife, children have less control than they do with plant life. Animals are capable of caring for themselves but benefit from the kindness of others. Choose a time of year when food for birds is scarce.

What to do
1. When you gather in a circle discuss the care and feeding of wildlife. If food for birds is scarce in winter in your area, discuss why this is so. Talk about various ways we can be kind to wildlife.

2. Invite the children to visit the science area to make special bird dinners.

3. Show the children how to roll pine cones or apples in lard or peanut butter, then dip them into bird seed.

4. Tie string around the bird meals leaving loose ends for hanging them up.

5. The children can also thread dry cereal hoops on to a piece of string. Roll the string in peanut butter and attach additional string for hanging.

6. Place the bird meals in the box as they are completed.

7. When the children have finished making the meals, gather in a circle to talk about their concern and kindness towards the birds. Take them outside and ask them to choose a nearby tree from which to hang or drape their meals. If possible, select a tree that can be seen from your school.

8. After hanging the meals on the tree, invite the children to join hands in a circle around the tree and repeat the following poem with you:
   Look little birds
   Here's something new
   To help you live
   A meal for you.

Want to do more?
Depending on where you live, choose an appropriate meal for a different type of wildlife.
• Read *The Very Hungry Caterpillar* by Eric Carle (Puffin Books).

Involving parents
Parents can also make BIRD DINNERS at home to hang from trees in their back gardens.

Growing Up

○ ✂

Looking after a baby, gentleness, consideration for others   Age *3+*

Things you will need
A four to ten-month-old baby
accompanied by a parent (if a real baby
is not available, substitute a doll)
A child's toy such as a soft toy, rattle,
ball
Baby clothes
Several baby care products

Children will be challenged to be
especially careful in the way they
respond to and handle a baby. They will
have to hold the child firmly without
squeezing too hard and support its body
properly, especially the head. This
special care will encourage children to
adjust to another person's needs.

What to do
1. Introduce the parent and baby to the
   children. Ask the parent to talk about
   the things they have brought along for
   the baby. If possible, allow the
   children to come up and touch the
   baby. Some children may even be
   allowed to hold the baby in their laps
   for a few moments.

2. Ask the children the following
   questions:
   *What things can you do that this
   baby cannot do?*
   *How are you different from this
   baby?*
   Summarize their comments as you go
   along. Emphasize the idea that
   children change as they grow up. As
   they grow, their abilities increase.

3. Discuss the type of care a baby needs
   to grow up healthy. What do mothers
   and fathers do to care for their babies?

4. Thank the visitors for coming to your
   class. With the parent's permission,
   invite the children to give the baby a
   gentle pat or hug as a friendly
   goodbye.

5. As a follow-up, ask the children to
   draw a picture of the baby. Collect
   the pictures and send them to the
   parent who made the visit.

Want to do more?
Children can bring their baby pictures to
show to the group.
• Read *Peepo!* by Janet and Allan
Ahlberg (Puffin Books).

Involving parents
Parents can show pre-schoolers their
baby toys or clothes if these were saved.
Parents can also tell the child how he or
she reacted to their care when being fed
or having a bath, for example.

Ouch

Looking after others

Age **3+**

Things you will need
Thick red paint and a small brush
Small, wet sponges and dry paper towels
(one for each child and teacher)
Plasters (one for each child and a few
extras)

The goal of this activity is to encourage
children to offer care to others, rather
than how to apply plasters correctly.
Young children may need help with
putting plasters on their partner, but
keep in mind that this is not a technical
lesson in first aid.

What to do
1. Ask the children if they have ever cut
   themselves. What is blood? Have they
   ever seen anyone bleed? What does
   'hurt' mean? Tell the children you
   have an activity in which they can
   help each other with a pretend OUCH.

2. Take out the paint and brush and tell
   them that you have a pretend cut.
   Take a little red paint and dab it on
   your finger. Say, *Oh, I have a pretend
   cut on my finger. Can someone help
   me?* Ask the volunteer helper to use

the sponge and paper towel to clean
and dry your 'ouch.' Then ask the
helper to put a plaster on your finger.

3. Ask the children to find a partner. Tell
   them that they will help each other
   with pretend OUCH's. Give a sponge,
   paper towel and plaster to each pair.
   Go around the circle, asking the
   partners which one is pretending to
   be hurt and which one is the helper.
   Hurt children indicate where they
   want the OUCH to be. Dab a small
   amount of paint on this spot. The
   helper then uses the sponge, paper
   towel and plaster to clean and protect
   the 'wound.'

4. Allow the children to switch roles and
   repeat the process once more.

Want to do more?
Ask an emergency medical technician to
visit your class and give a few simple
first aid lessons.
• Read *I'm Falling to Bits* by Tedd
Arnold (Macdonald Young Books).

Involving parents
The next time a parent has a simple cut,
they can involve their child in
administering first aid. Even though
parents may perform first aid faster and
better, asking children to help
strengthens their self-esteem and gives
them practice in looking after others.

Know See

Helping, consideration for others

○

Age *3+*

Things you will need
Two blindfolds

By blindfolding yourself, you challenge children to relate to you with words and touch rather than visual cues. Teacher, look at this! will no longer work. Be sure a helper or another teacher will supervise your children before attempting this activity. If you do not feel happy about promising to keep the blindfold on, do not introduce this activity. Avoid giving in to the temptation to peep. Challenge yourself to experience this sensory deprivation.

What to do
1. Tell the children you would like to find out what it would be like to be a pretend 'blind' person in their class. Discuss and clarify any misconceptions they have about blindness. Emphasize that you plan to wear the blindfold for the morning but can remove it if necessary. Tell them that you will need their help while you wear the blindfold. Invite them to try wearing one for a short while, too.

2. Put on the blindfold and describe what you hear, smell, feel around you.

3. Keep the blindfold on as long as you can. Share your thoughts and feelings with the children while wearing the blindfold. Ask for their help when needed.

4. When you are ready to remove the blindfold, gather the children in a circle and share your experiences.

Want to do more?
If you do this activity with older children, let a volunteer take you for a walk outside in a protected area.
• Read *Is That What Friends Do?* by Marjorie Newman, illustrated by Peter Bowman (Hutchinson).

Involving parents
Parents can let their children take them for a blind walk around the inside of their home.

Lotion Motion

Gentleness, cooperation

○
Age **4+**

Things you will need
Hand cream or lotion

This activity provides children with a fun way to make gentle contact with each other. It is good to do this activity after the children have washed their hands.

What to do
1. Ask the children to find a partner and sit facing each other. Go around the room and put hand cream or lotion in each child's hand. Ask the children to find out how the lotion feels by rubbing their hands together. After a few moments, ask them to join hands with their partner. Encourage them to explore each other's hands in a massaging motion.

2. Call the group together and ask everyone to make a close, friendly circle. All the children can reach their hands into the middle of the circle and touch each other's hands. Pour extra lotion over their hands and encourage everyone to explore the different textures. Emphasize gentle contact. Encourage motion by suggesting that the hands on the bottom move to the top in a repeated cycle.

Want to do more?
Instead of lotion, place one small lump of soft playdough in each child's hands. Can they knead the dough together?

Involving parents
Describe this activity for parents to try with their children at home. LOTION MOTION can be fun with feet, too.

How Are You?   ○

Looking after others, gentleness   *Age* 4+

Things you will need
Blanket
Pillow
Flannel
Bowl with a small amount of warm
water

A relatively complex act like looking
after someone can be broken down into
its fundamental components. Cooling a
person's forehead with a flannel or
covering another with a blanket are
simple caring skills young children can
learn and practise. At fourteen months,
children will pat and stroke someone in
distress. Beyond eighteen months, their
caretaking becomes more sophisticated,
including hugging, seeking adult help
and finding comforting objects such as
blankets and toys. In this activity,
provide simple, easily understood
explanations of the causes and
consequences of being ill or hurt. Avoid
using the word 'bug' to refer to bacteria
or viruses. Describe and discuss
symptoms of illness like sore throat,
cough, fever, upset stomach. Provide
factual reassurance to children who are
frightened about an illness or accident.

What to do
1. Ask the children if they have ever
   been unwell. Take a few moments to
   discuss times when they were ill.

2. Introduce the activity with the
   following story:

   Once upon a time in Butterberry Hill,
   Amy became very ill. Her mummy
   brought her a blanket and pillow so
   she could lie down. Because Amy
   was ill, her temperature went up, and
   she became very hot. Her mummy

and daddy took a damp flannel and
gently washed her face to make her
feel cooler. After two days of rest and
loving care, Amy felt better and could
go to school once again. The End.

3. Tell the children that you have an
   activity in which they will pretend to
   care for someone who is ill. Ask for a
   volunteer to pretend to be ill. Ask the
   volunteer to go to the centre of the
   circle and lie down on their back. Ask
   them to point to someone who can
   help them.

4. Ask the helper to put the pillow under
   the 'ill' child's head and to cover
   them with a blanket. Then set the
   bowl and flannel near the sick child's
   head. Ask them to close their eyes
   and then ask the helper to gently
   sponge their forehead and cheeks
   with the flannel dipped in warm
   water.

5. Ask for another volunteer to be the
   pretend sick person and continue with
   other rounds of gentle caring.

Want to do more?
You can set up a make-believe 'hospital'
in the dressing-up area where two or
three children pretend to be ill.

Involving parents
Parents can ask children to place a
damp flannel on their forehead when
they have a headache or need to relax.

Hospital Gifts

Generosity

○ ✂

Age **4+**

Things you will need
Paper
Crayons
Large envelope

Activities like HOSPITAL GIFTS empower children to be kind to others. Young children have little understanding of suffering in other people. At this age, the emphasis should be on relating their personal experience to that of others. Can they remember when they were ill? What happened? Well, here is someone who is ill. Let's be kind to him.

What to do
1. Contact the paediatric or geriatric ward of a local hospital to see if they would like drawings from children in your class.

2. Ask the children to describe what being 'ill' means. Direct the discussion to hospitals and hospital experiences. How do people in hospital feel? Discuss how it feels to be separated from family and home.

3. Tell the children that they have the chance to be kind to some sick children (or elders). Go to the art area and distribute paper and crayons. Ask the children to draw a special picture for someone who is in hospital.

4. Emphasize the positive feelings that children or the elderly may have when they receive the pictures. Place the pictures in an envelope and send them to your contact at the hospital.

Want to do more?
Instead of sending the drawings, you can visit the institution and drop them off.
• You can substitute a nursing home for the hospital and give the pictures to the residents. Elders can draw their own pictures to give to the children.
• Read *Arthur's Chicken Pox* by Marc Brown (Red Fox).

Involving parents
Parents and children can cooperate on a family drawing to send to an elderly family member who is not feeling well.

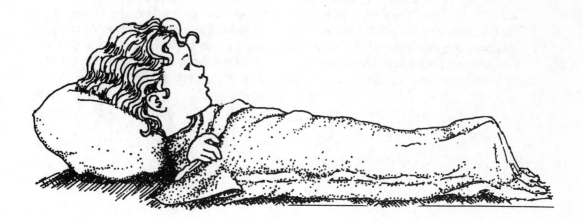

Rescue Chain

Rescue, cooperation

○ ✳

Age **4+**

Things you will need
Chalk or rope (optional)

Identifying circumstances that are threatening or dangerous is an early step in the development of courage in children. Even though very young children are not capable of real rescues, role playing this aspect of kindness establishes its value.

What to do
1. As an introduction to the activity, tell the children the following story:

   Once upon a time, Penelope Pig decided to go skating on the frozen pond near Butterberry Hill. All of her friends told her, Don't go skating. The ice is thin, and you might fall in. But Penelope ignored them and went skating anyway. When she was skating in the middle of the pond, the ice broke, and Penelope fell right into the icy cold water. She was trapped in the ice and was sinking fast. When her friends saw her, they wanted to go out on the ice to pull her out. But if they did that, then they would fall in, too. They decided to make a rescue chain. Each person held onto the next person's hand as they stretched out to take hold and pull Penelope out. The End.

2. Ask the children whether they would like to pretend to be like Penelope's friends and rescue her from the icy water. Ask for a volunteer to be Penelope Pig. The rest of the children will make the chain.

3. In a large outdoor space, identify a boundary between the shore and the water. You can draw a line with chalk or stretch out a rope. Place Penelope, sitting on the ground, a sufficient distance from the shore to require a slight stretch in the chain to reach her.

4. Tell the rescuers they have only a few minutes to save Penelope. One rescuer is the anchor, who must remain on shore. You can ask this person to hold onto the branch of a tree or the bar of a jungle gym. The rest of the children make a line, hand in hand, to stretch out to take Penelope's hand. If the line breaks, everyone in the part of the line not connected to the shore will have to sit down to be rescued, too.

5. Ask the children to begin. Cheer them on as they form a line and begin stretching toward Penelope. After a few rounds of the game, talk with the children about the dangers present at a lake or pond at different times of the year.

Want to do more?

To add challenge, decrease the amount of time allowed for the rescue and increase the distance between the shore and Penelope. Obviously, Penelope must not be beyond the extreme range of the rescue chain.

• Another version is to designate two children as the ends of the chain, one the anchor, one the grabber. Play by the same rules as above but blindfold the grabber to simulate a night rescue.

Involving parents

While the family watches television, parents can talk with their children about characters who 'rescue' others. They can use words like 'brave' or 'courageous' in their conversations.

Food for the Hungry

Generosity

⭕

Age **4+**

Things you will need
Paper
Several tins of vegetables, soup or fruit
to serve as extras

Young children who have never known
prolonged hunger cannot comprehend
the experience of those who have.
Young children can, however, understand that they are doing something to
help others by bringing food to school.

What to do
1. Contact your local church or
   homeless shelter to make arrange-
   ments for bringing in food donations.

2. Write a brief letter to the parents of
   your children describing your food
   drive. Tell them the date on which
   you would like the children to bring
   one tin of food to the school.

3. When the children are gathered in a
   circle, discuss briefly the fact that
   some children and their families in
   your community do not have enough
   to eat. Tell the children that you will
   send a letter home to their parents
   asking them to donate a tin of food
   for their children to give to the
   hungry.

4. Discuss why good nutritious food is
   important and suggest different types
   of food that are needed.

5. On the day of the food collection,
   give a tin of food to the children who
   did not bring one from home. When
   all the children have arrived, gather in
   a circle and ask everyone to bring
   their tins of food. Go around the
   circle, each child identifying the food
   they have brought. Thank each child
   individually. Briefly describe how a
   hungry person would react to the food
   they have brought. You might say
   something like, *Oh, those peaches
   will taste so good. Peaches will help
   make a hungry person healthy.*

6. Try to arrange for your class to take
   the food to the church or shelter. If
   this is not possible, perhaps someone
   from the church or shelter might visit
   your class to collect the food and talk
   to the children.

Want to do more?
Instead of food, the children can bring in
a spare toy for distribution to
disadvantaged children at Christmas.
• Read *Solo* by Paul Geraghty
(Hutchinson).

Involving parents
Parents can involve their children in
deciding which food to provide. What
food would be the best to choose? A tin
of peaches is better and more nutritious
than a bag of sweets.

Kindness Coupons

Generosity, helping

○ ✄

Age **4+**

Things you will need

12 x 20 cm (5" x 8") cards
Pen
Crayons or markers
Envelopes

In our materialistic society, children typically associate gifts with purchases from a shop. But a gift can also be a service — like helping someone clean up — or a creation — like a drawing or painting. This activity provides a balance to the commercial messages children see in the media.

What to do

1. Introduce the activity when they are gathered in a circle by asking the children to identify things other members of their family would like to receive as gifts. What is a gift? Emphasize that something kind that you do for someone is also a gift. Ask children for examples of what they could do that would be 'kind' to other family members. Offer examples from your own experience.

2. Tell the children you will set up a KINDNESS COUPON shop in the art area. (You may have to explain what a coupon is.) They will come to the shop to make coupons which they can use as gifts for family members.

3. Ask each child to name what they can do that would be kind to other family members. Help the child identify simple activities like 'a gentle hug,' or 'singing a song' or 'helping clean up the kitchen.' Try to identify a couple of kind acts for each family member.

4. Write each idea on a separate 12cm x 20cm (5" x 8") card. Ask the children to decorate the cards with crayons or magic markers. They might draw a picture of themselves offering to do a kind activity.

5. Put each card into an envelope with the family member's name on the outside. Explain the activity to parents when they arrive and ask them to keep the envelopes for a future holiday or birthday.

Want to do more?

Read *Oh, Little Jack* by Inga Moore (Walker Books).

Involving parents

Parents can give their children their own set of KINDNESS COUPONS. For example, one might say, If you give me this coupon before dinner, I will take you out for an ice cream. Parents should only make promises in the KINDNESS COUPONS that they can keep. The children can only cash one coupon a day.

Blind Kind

Helping, consideration for others

○
Age **4+**

Things you will need
Blindfold for each child
Small lunch bag for each child
An interesting classroom object placed
in each bag such as a small stuffed
animal, a block, a piece from a jigsaw
puzzle

This introduction to using a blindfold
reduces some of the apprehension
children may feel by keeping them
seated and allowing them to stay in
control. Success with this activity is
necessary before introducing other
activities that involve blindfolds. The
teacher models gentle helping.

What to do
1. Ask the children to close their eyes
for a few moments. Talk with them
about what it means to be blind. How
would they feel?

2. Show the blindfolds to the children.
Show them how to put one on. While
wearing a blindfold, describe what
your other senses are telling you.
What do you hear? What can you
touch around you? What can you
smell? Take the blindfold off and give
one to each child.

3. Tell the children that you would like
them to pretend they cannot see. You
would like to be kind and give them
something to touch, smell or hear.
Place a closed bag directly in front of
each child. Invite the children to put
on their blindfolds. Emphasize that
they should remain seated.

4. When everyone is ready, tell them to
open their bags to find what you
wanted to show them. Encourage
them to smell, feel and listen to the
sounds the object makes. The
emphasis here is to experience rather
than identify the object.

5. After a minute, tell them they can
remove their blindfolds to see what
was in the bag.

6. Do not force any child to wear the
blindfold. Some may need to watch
others before they feel safe doing so.
If they prefer, children can simply
close their eyes.

Want to do more?
If children are ready to be blindfolded
for longer, ask them to pass their object
to the child on their right. After about 30
seconds of exploration, they can pass
again. Give directions before they put on
the blindfolds.
• Read *The Very Quiet Cricket* by Eric
Carle (Puffin Books).

Involving parents
Parents can introduce BLIND KIND at
home, taking turns with their children
to wear the blindfold.

Wishing Well

Generosity, consideration for others

○
Age **4+**

Things you will need
None

The wishes you suggest in this activity can be pure fantasy, or they may reflect your knowledge of what a child really wants to have or do. Whichever is the case, make your wishes for all the children in your group equally important.

What to do
1. Ask the children if they know what a 'wish' means. Talk about a few wishes you might have for yourself. Identify someone you care about in your family and tell the children what you would wish for them. Can the children think of wishes they could make for themselves or others?

2. Ask the children to repeat the following poem with you:
   If my mind was a wishing well,
   I'd find a wish that I could tell —
   Something you could have to do
   To make you happy all day
   through.

3. After one full verse, describe a wish you would like to make for one of the children in your group. For example, you might say, *Sarah, my wish for you is that every morning ten lovely teddy bears wake you up with gentle hugs and by singing songs.*

4. Then ask the group to chant the lines of the poem with you. Ask a volunteer to offer a wish to someone else. Repeat the cycle and continue as long as the children are interested. Be sure to stop before the children become tired. Give the children who did not have a turn the opportunity to offer wishes at another time.

Want to do more?
How about wishes for the entire group? For example, you can say, I wish our whole group was in the mountains, singing songs around a beautiful waterfall.
• Read *Peter in Blueberry Land* by Elsa Beskow (Floris Books).

Involving parents
Parents can describe their wishes for their children as well as other family members. Send home copies of the poem for parents to repeat with their children. Parents can be imaginative in their wishes. They might suggest shoes that make their children fly or a magic sack of toys that would never become empty.

Give a Lift

Looking after others, gentleness   O

Age 4+

Things you will need
Nothing

Children whose arms are lifted experience gentle support from their peers. Those who do the lifting have the opportunity to look after another person very gently.

What to do
1. Talk briefly with the children about the meaning of gentleness. Invite the children to participate in a simple activity which allows them to be kind and gentle to other children in the class.

2. Ask a volunteer to come to the centre of the circle and lie down, letting all their muscles relax, just like a rag doll. Gently lift each of the child's arms and legs, one at a time. Talk about being gentle as you do so. Ask the child not to help you by lifting their arms or legs. You will do the lifting.

3. Invite other children to carry out the same gentle action with the child's arms and legs. After several children have taken turns lifting, ask for another volunteer to pretend to be a rag doll.

Want to do more?
Play the rag doll yourself and invite children — perhaps two at a time — to lift your arms. Praise children for lifting gently and slowly.

Involving parents
Parents can lie on the floor or the bed while their children gently lift their arms.

Flower Power

Generosity

✂ ○

Age **4+**

Things you will need

Pre-cut paper flower stems, leaves, buds
Small bottles of glue
Crayons
Construction paper

Be aware of the give-and-take going on in this activity. Who gives but does not receive? Who refuses to participate? Do not force children to give any of their flowers. Generosity should be sincere. Give children a choice.

What to do

1. Invite the children to make special flowers at the table in the art area table. Pass round the materials and demonstrate how the various pieces can be pasted onto construction paper to make a flower. Ask the children to make flowers on two sheets of paper. They can use crayons to illustrate additional details. Make flowers on two sheets of construction paper yourself.

2. When the flower-making activity is completed, and the glue has dried, ask the children to bring their flowers to the circle. Discuss with them the feelings that people have when someone is kind and gives them something. Tell them that you would like to give your flowers to two children in the class.

3. After giving the flowers to two children, ask, Would anyone like to give one or both of their flowers to another person in our group? The children then take turns giving the flowers they made to others, if they choose to. Ask the children to thank those who give them flowers.

Want to do more?

Look for opportunities to encourage generosity in everyday relationships in your classroom.
• Read *Angelina's Christmas* by Katherine Holabird, illustrated by Helen Craig (Puffin Books).

Involving parents

Send home several sheets of construction paper of different colours and encourage parents to make flowers to give to their children.

Birds in the Trees

Protection, cooperation, consideration for others   *Age* **4+**

Things you will need
Music

There are no losers in this variation of
MUSICAL CHAIRS. Instead of children
sitting on the sidelines, everyone
remains involved. Emphasis is on
cooperation rather than competition.

What to do
1. Talk with the children about
   protection. Steer the conversation
   toward the idea of shelter as a form of
   protection. Where do birds and other
   creatures find protection when there is
   a thunderstorm? How do our homes
   protect and keep us safe?

2. Tell the children that you have a
   protection game for them to play.
   Some of them will pretend to be trees,
   and others will be birds flying through
   the forest. When the music plays, the
   weather is nice, and the birds can fly.
   When the music stops, the thunderstorm begins, and the birds will have
   to find shelter under the outstretched
   branches of the trees. As time goes

by, however, there will be fewer trees
and more birds. The birds will have to
do their best to huddle under the
remaining branches.

3. Ask for a quarter of the group to
   volunteer to pretend to be birds. The
   remaining children are trees. Arrange
   the trees to make a forest, leaving
   sufficient room for the birds to fly
   through safely. Tell the trees that they
   must remain in place. When the
   music stops, they should stretch out
   their arms to provide branches for the
   birds. The birds seek shelter under the
   branches of any tree.

4. Begin playing the music. Encourage
   the birds to fly around the forest.
   When the music stops, tell them to
   find shelter under or near the branches of a tree. Emphasize the idea of
   finding protection under the trees.

5. After each round, ask one tree to
   become a bird. Continue for several
   rounds until there is only one tree left.
   If the birds cannot touch a branch,
   they can huddle close to each other.
   Finish by making all the children birds
   and yourself the last tree.

Want to do more?
Play two different musical instruments to
signal nice weather and a thunderstorm.
• Read *The Story of the Root Children*
by Sibylle von Olfers (Floris Books).

Involving parents
Parents can take their children for a
walk in the neighbourhood or a nearby
park to look for the 'homes' that shelter
and protect various types of wildlife.

Let's Be Generous

Generosity

○

Age **4+**

Things you will need
Bowl of biscuits or small gifts

This activity can be difficult for children accustomed to helping themselves. Make sure they understand the rule that the only way they can get a biscuit is if someone gives one to them. This is always a very useful activity, but it is especially effective when children are getting to know each other.

What to do
1. Set the bowl in the centre of the circle or in your lap, and ask the children if they know what 'giving' and 'generous' mean. Briefly discuss how you felt when someone gave something to you. Comment that since the children in the class are learning to become friends, you would like to give them the opportunity to give something to each other.

2. Take something out of the bowl and say, *I would like to be kind and generous to Simon.* After giving the gift, ask children if they would like to be kind and generous to someone. A volunteer then goes to the centre of the circle, selects a gift — such as a biscuit — and chooses a recipient. Repeat with other volunteers until all the children have received something.

3. You may have to take a second turn to give a 'gift' to someone who has been overlooked by the others. Do this with great tact to avoid embarrassing the child. Remind children that giving something to someone is a way of showing affection, showing that you like them. No one should leave the group without having received at least one share.

Want to do more?
Use words or actions as a form of kindness. For example, you can hug a child or say something kind.
• Read *The Toymaker* by Martin Waddell, Illustrated by Terry Milne (Walker Books).

Involving parents
Encourage parents to provide opportunities for their children to be generous.

Wonder Wands

Gentleness, respect/encouragement

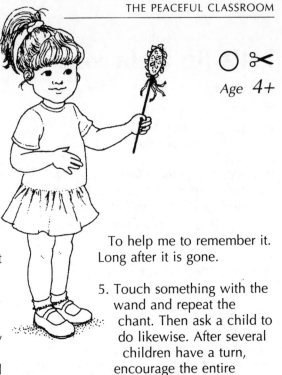

Age **4+**

Things you will need
A wooden rod or stick approximately
350 mm (14") long for each child
Decorative art materials (stars, glitter,
ribbon, felt tip pens, etc.)
Glue

This activity encourages children to
notice, appreciate and remember what
they think is beautiful around them.

What to do
1. Ask the children to describe what
   they think 'beauty' means. Can they
   identify something they think is
   beautiful? Point out that people find
   different things to be beautiful.
   Provide a few examples of people
   who have different opinions about
   what is beautiful.

2. Show them a wooden rod. Tell them
   that they are going to decorate the rod
   to make pretend magic WONDER
   WANDS. Describe the materials set out
   in the art area. We can pretend that
   these WONDER WANDS are like magic.
   Gently touching something we think
   is beautiful with the wand will help us
   remember that beautiful thing for a
   long time afterwards.

3. At the art area, work beside the
   children to make your own WONDER
   WAND.

4. When the wands are completed and
   the glue firmly dried, call the children
   together to show off their creations.
   Teach them the following poem to
   recite as they gently touch something
   they think is beautiful.
   Here is a beautiful thing;
   I will touch it with my hand

To help me to remember it.
Long after it is gone.

5. Touch something with the
   wand and repeat the
   chant. Then ask a child to
   do likewise. After several
   children have a turn,
   encourage the entire
   group to explore the
   surrounding area with their
   WONDER WANDS.

6. At the end of the school day, tell the
   children that they can take their
   WONDER WANDS home. They can
   bring them back to school another
   day if they wish. Before dismissing the
   children, describe several things that
   you touched with your WONDER
   WAND and why you want to
   remember these things. Encourage
   children to identify what they
   touched.

Want to do more?
Consider touching each child in your
class with the wand while reciting the
poem.
• Read *The Whales' Song* by Dyan
Sheldon and Gary Blythe (Red Fox).

Involving parents
Children can take their WONDER WANDS
home to show their parents. They also
can teach their parents the poem and
show them how to make wands.

No Stranger to Danger

Rescue   ○

Age **4+**

Things you will need
Five pictures from magazines of things
likely to be dangerous, e.g., knife, fire,
sharp tools, electrical socket, bottle of
detergent, broken glass
Five pictures of things likely to be safe,
e.g., harmless insect, kitten, book, teddy
bear, chair

Courage depends on evaluating danger
and choosing an effective response.
Understanding why an object or
situation may be dangerous is an
important basis for intelligent action.

What to do
1. Talk to the children about the idea of
   keeping oneself and others safe. Ask
   the children for their ideas about what
   is safe and what is dangerous. Make
   sure they understand that 'dangerous'
   means that something might hurt you
   if you are not careful.

2. When you think the children
   understand these concepts, show
   them a pair of pictures, one showing
   something 'safe,' the other something
   'dangerous.' Ask, *Which of these two
   things is safer than the other?* When
   one child responds, ask them to tell
   the group what makes one thing more
   safe or dangerous than another.

Want to do more?
Read *Smudge, The Little Lost Lamb* by
James Herriot, illustrated by Ruth Brown
(Picture Piper).

Involving parents
Parents and children can go on a search
throughout the house to find objects that
are possibly dangerous, such as a knife,
electric socket, matches.

Staying Safe

Rescue

O

Age **4+**

Things you will need
Five or more pictures of potentially dangerous places, e.g., busy street, beach, bathroom, kitchen, car, stairs, or cliff.

Differentiating between reasonable and unreasonable danger is an important part of courage. No matter how unreasonable we think they may be, children's fears are part of their experience of the world. Without belittling their fears, we should encourage them to evaluate whether a fear is reasonable.

What to do
1. Ask the children to tell you what they think 'safe' and 'dangerous' and 'careful' mean. Can they give examples of these terms? Tell them you are going to show pictures of places that could be dangerous if a person were not careful.

2. Show them one picture and ask, What could be dangerous about this place? What do we have to do to be careful? After the children give some ideas, summarize and add key points that you want them to consider.

3. Go back to each picture and create a circumstance in which children see a younger brother or sister acting recklessly in that place. For example, You get up in the morning to make yourself some breakfast. You see your little brother climbing on to the kitchen sink to open the cupboard. He pulls out some of your mother's medicine and tries to remove the lid. What do you do? Encourage the children to identify as many responses to the situation as possible. Introduce

the term 'rescue' to describe their attempt to keep the young person from being hurt.

Want to do more?
Instead of using pictures, verbally recreate a wide variety of situations.

Involving parents
Parents can take their children for a walk in and around the house and neighbourhood to find places that could be dangerous. They can discuss how children can keep themselves safe at each location.

Ship in the Night

Helping, rescue, cooperation

○ Age **4+**

Things you will need
One blindfold

This activity places greater demands on children by asking them to move with a blindfold on. Movement within the circle ensures safety and provides security for the blindfolded child.

What to do
1. Tell the children you have a blindfold game for them to play. Begin with this story:

   Once upon a time, not far from Butterberry Hill, there was a boat that became lost at night. There was no moon overhead, and it was as dark as could be. None of the sailors on the boat could see. There was a storm coming, and they had to find a safe place to land. Amy knew the people on the boat were lost. So she walked out to the beach and shouted the ship's name over and over again. The kind North Wind carried her voice out to the boat, and the sailors steered towards the sound to safety. The End.

2. The children will have the opportunity to pretend to be the boat and the rescuer.

3. Everyone joins hands to make a circle. Ask for a volunteer to be the ship. The ship goes to the centre of the circle and chooses a child in the circle to be 'Amy' (the rescuer). Blindfold the ship. Ask the circle of children to rotate around the ship while singing, *Here we go, around and around — find your partner by their sound.*

4. Both the rotation and the chant stop at the same time. Standing in the circle, 'Amy' begins saying the ship's name, over and over again, while the ship tries to approach and make contact with her. Other children in the circle remain quiet as they protect the ship from leaving the circle. Any child who is touched can gently direct the ship in the correct direction.

Want to do more?
To simplify the activity, be the North Wind who gently steers the ship toward Amy. The ship's task is also easier if the circle is smaller.
• To increase the difficulty, the other children in the circle can make rainstorm noises to complicate Amy's rescue.
• Read *The Mousehole Cat* by Antonia Barber, illustrated by Nicola Bayley (Walker Books).

Involving parents
Parents can blindfold their child and then begin quietly calling the child from the other end of the room. Parents and children can take turns switching roles.

Know Talk   ◯

Helping, consideration for others   Age **4+**

Things you will need
None

Be prepared to experience some frustration when trying to communicate without words with children. As with other sensory deprivation activities, working through their frustration is an important part of the experience.

What to do
1. Ask the children to tell you why being able to talk is important. How would they feel if they could never talk with words? Mention that some people cannot talk because the parts of their bodies that make a voice do not work correctly.

2. Introduce the idea of sign language: talking with hands and other parts of the body. Demonstrate several examples and ask the children to identify what you are trying to tell them:
    Nod head for yes
    Shake head fro no
    Shake a tight fist and make an angry face
    Wave goodbye
    (Extend both arms as an invitation to hug.)

3. Tell the children that you want to find out what it would be like to be a person who cannot talk in their classroom. When you finish describing this activity, you will pretend for the rest of the morning that you cannot talk. If you have something to tell them, you will say it with your hands and facial expression.

4. For the rest of the morning, if speaking is necessary, motion to another teacher or helper to talk for you. At the end of your experiment, discuss with the children what happened.

Want to do more?
Invite the children to explore how they make sounds. Ask them to touch their throats while making different sounds, or talk while pinching their noses shut, or talk with their tongues sticking out. Emphasize that many different parts of the body contribute to making speech sounds.
• Invite a sign language expert to visit your class and teach the children a few basics of that language.

Involving parents
Parents can play a similar game of sign language with their children. Older children can try signing an entire conversation at a meal time.

See For You

Helping, consideration for others

Things you will need
One small paper bag and one blindfold for every pair of children

This activity adds more uncertainty to the experience of wearing a blindfold. Wearers will have to be patient while their helpers provide them with objects to explore. Children will have the opportunity to both receive and give assistance.

What to do
1. Tell the children you have another kindness activity involving a blindfold for them to try. One child will wear the blindfold while their partner finds things for them to feel, hear and smell.

2. Ask each child to find a partner. Give the pair a blindfold and a paper bag. Ask them who will be the helper and who will wear the blindfold.

3. Ask the helpers to find four interesting objects for their blindfolded partners to feel, hear and smell. Ask them to put the objects into the bag and keep what they select a secret.

4. When they return, help them put the blindfold on their partners. When the children are ready, the helpers can open the bag and give one object to the child to explore. After about 30 seconds, tell them they can hand over the next thing they found.

5. To reduce distraction, discourage children from talking too much during the activity.

6. When all the objects have been shared, the children can reverse roles.

Want to do more?
Show the children how to hand something gently to someone who cannot see. Blindfolded children can be startled by a partner who drops objects into their hands.
•Emphasize the idea that sometimes people do not want help. Blind people, for example, learn to explore the world and find things on their own. Avoid creating the impression that disabled people are completely dependent on others.
• To simplify the activity, prepare bags ahead of time with three or four items for children to hand to their partners.

Involving parents
Parents can repeat the activity with their children at home, taking turns being the helper.

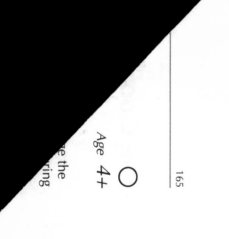

their best to respond to the problem, whether it involves standing up to a bully or touching a strange looking insect. These moments of courage contribute to a child's sense of personal power and self-esteem. Be aware of these moments of personal courage demonstrated by children.

What to do

1. Begin the activity with the following story:

Once upon a time in Butterberry Hill, Amy felt very sad. Her little dog Sparkles was missing. Sparkles didn't come home for dinner. Amy looked everywhere in Butterberry Hill but could not find him. She looked on and around Moonsweep Mountain. Sparkles was not there. Then...ugh! She went to the edge of Stinky Swamp. There in the middle of the swamp on a little island that stuck up from the slurpy, dirty water was Sparkles. He looked so sad. He couldn't leave, though, because his little island was surrounded by the Grumpy Goonfallas. They were hungry, too. They were asleep, but Sparkles was too afraid to leave. As long as he stayed on the little island, the Grumpy Goonfallas could not get him. Well, Amy saw this and knew she would have to get Sparkles before

the Goonfallas woke up. So she said some brave words to herself: 'When you are afraid and think you might cry, say *I will do what I can; I will stay and try.'*

Very carefully, so as not to touch any of the sleeping Grumpy Goonfallas, Amy tiptoed through the slurpy water [mime and exaggerate]. When she arrived at the island, she picked up Sparkles and tiptoed back to the shore. Then she quickly ran over Moonsweep Mountain right back to Butterberry Hill. Whew! She had rescued Sparkles. He was so happy. And hungry too! The End.

2. Ask the children if they know what 'rescue' means. Take a few moments to discuss their ideas.

3. Set the rug in a corner of the room. The rug is the small island in the middle of Stinky Swamp. Place the rope about three metres/ten feet from the island to mark where the swamp water ends. Set the stuffed animal (poor little Sparkles) on the rug. Place blocks (Grumpy Goonfallas) between the shore and the island. The Grumpy Goonfallas are sleeping. With one touch, though, they might wake up!

4. Invite the children to rescue Sparkles by walking around the Grumpy Goon-fallas, picking up Sparkles and return-ing to shore. A child who touches a block must go to the island and wait to be rescued by another child.

Want to do more?
If you do not have large building blocks, use rolled up towels or folded blankets for the Grumpy Goonfallas.
• Increase the difficulty by increasing the number of Grumpy Goonfallas and setting them closer together.
• Instead of a stuffed animal, a child can pretend to be Sparkles.

Involving parents
Parents can introduce rescue themes when they play with their children. They can also talk to them about courageous actions reported in the media.

The Touch Toe Path

Helping, gentleness

Age **4+**

Things you will need

Various textured materials: a square of perspex with no sharp edges, carpet samples, sandpaper, a square of plywood with no splinters, a wet towel placed on a plastic bin liner, a dry towel, small stones spread out on a large baking tray, four bricks sandwiched together (watch out for stubbed toes), a piece of furry cloth, a sheet of tin foil, an artificial grass mat, a small folded blanket, leaves spread out on a large baking tray, a large sheet of paper
Blindfolds
Two chairs

By guiding their partners down a path, children help someone dependent on them in a controlled, safe situation. Encourage partners to walk slowly down the path.

What to do

1. Create a path with several different surfaces and set a chair at both ends of the path.

2. Gather the children in a circle near the path. Tell them that you have created a TOUCH TOE PATH for them to walk down. They must walk with their shoes and socks off, with a blindfold on and with a partner helping them.

3. The children select partners and queue behind the chair at the beginning of the path. One child from the first pair sits and removes their shoes and socks and is blindfolded. Emphasize to the helpers that they should gently and slowly lead their blindfolded partners down the path. Show them how to put one hand on the partner's back or shoulder while holding the other hand. Ask them to watch their partners' feet and tell them when they need to move to avoid stubbing his toes.

4. When the children finish the walk, their partners should help them sit in the chair at the end of the path and remove the blindfold. They can return to the beginning and repeat the activity, switching roles.

Want to do more?

Older children can take partners for barefoot walks in the playground during warm weather.

Involving parents

Parents and children can take each other on TOUCH TOE WALKS around the house.

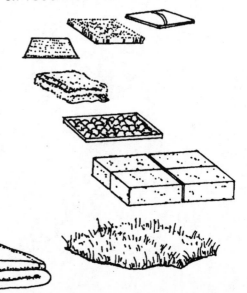

Get Well

Generosity, encouragement, association, conversation

○ ✂

Age *4+*

Things you will need
Paper
Crayons
Watercolours or felt tip pens

Drawing children's attention to someone else's feelings and perceptions is an important step in encouraging them to move from thinking only of themselves to thinking about the whole group. To offer relevant encouragement it is necessary to understand another person's goals.

What to do
1. When you find out that a child is too ill to come to class, tell the parent about this activity and ask if the child is well enough to receive a telephone call. If not, skip the call and just do the drawings. Arrange for the parent to pick them up or for someone, perhaps another parent, to drop them off at the child's home.

2. Gather the children into a circle early in the day and ask them if they know who is missing. Talk about why the child is absent. Take a few moments to let the children talk about the various illnesses they have had.

3. Tell the group that [name the child] is probably unhappy that they could not come to school. Ask the children to think about what they might be able to do to cheer the child up. Invite them to visit the art area to draw special pictures to be collected and sent to them. You can write special messages from the children directly on the drawings. Let the children decide what they want to draw.

4. When the drawings are completed, gather the children around a phone. Tell them you would like to call the sick child and let them say some kind words. Ask them what they think would be kind to say. Make the call and let each child who wishes have a minute of conversation.

Want to do more?
Each picture can be a little story that the children make up as they draw it. The teacher can write the story as it is told and attach it to the drawing.

Involving parents
Parents and children can pick someone to call on the telephone who is not feeling well or might benefit from the personal contact. Talk about this person before you call. After the call, emphasize the good feelings it created. Ask parents to think about the type of encouragement they give their children. How do they praise their children, when they try hard to succeed?

Sheet Carry

Gentleness, rescue, cooperate

○

Age **4+**

Things you will need
One large, sturdy bed sheet or blanket
Two small rugs

Avoid becoming too frightening when role playing rescue and protection activities.

What to do
1. Talk for a few moments with the children about the meaning of 'danger' and 'rescue.' Give examples of each. Introduce the activity with the following story:

   Once upon a time in Butterberry Hill, Penelope Pig was watching television when she suddenly smelled smoke. Oh no! There must be a fire in the house. Penelope was so scared. She ran down the steps to get outside, but then she fell and hurt herself. She could not get up to walk out of the house. Sam and Amy saw the smoke and called the fire station. When the fire fighters arrived, they found Penelope and carried her out of the house on a blanket. The End.

2. Tell the children you have a similar rescue activity for them to try. One child will pretend to be Penelope who is hurt and unable to leave the burning building; other children will pretend to be fire fighters who make the rescue. Fire fighters will have to carry Penelope to safety on a sheet.

3. Ask for a volunteer to pretend to be Penelope and six to eight children to be rescuers. Take Penelope to one side of the room and ask her to lie down on one of the small rugs and pretend to be injured. Tell the group

that this rug is inside her house. Penelope cannot move or help the rescuers in any way.

4. Take the fire fighters to the opposite side of the room and give them the sheet. Lay the second rug down and tell the group that this is the hospital. Their task is to run over to Penelope, stretch the sheet out on the ground next to her and gently lift her up and onto the sheet. Then they should gather around the sheet to pick it up and bring her to the hospital. Demonstrate, if necessary. The remaining children can cheer the rescuers on.

5. Stay with the rescuers to make sure Penelope is carried safely. Be especially careful to protect the child's head when they are lifted onto the sheet.

6. Provide opportunities for all children to participate in the rescue.

Want to do more?
Read *Fabian Youngpig Sails the World* by Ingrid Ostheeren, illustrated by Serena Romanelli (North-South Books, US).

Involving parents
Create a similar play situation at home with parents 'rescuing' the child from various dangerous situations. Parents can talk about a time in their lives when they did something courageous.

Sad Person

Generosity, recognition of emotions, problem solving   ○ Age **4+**

Things you will need
Bowl of finger food liked by children in your group (biscuits, raisins, crisps, etc.)
Cloth to cover bowl

Even though children are not giving away something they own, the act of choosing and handing something to another is important practice for generosity. Make sure children are aware of the other person's pleased response when they receive a 'gift.'

What to do
1. Place the items to be distributed in the bowl. Cover the bowl with cloth.

2. Ask the children, What friendly things can people do for you when you feel sad? Emphasize offerings like hugs, playing a game, taking you somewhere, in addition to material things like buying a gift or making you something good to eat.

3. Tell the children that you are going to give them an opportunity to be generous to somebody who is pretending to be sad. Set the bowl in front of you and remove the cloth.

4. Ask if anyone would like to pretend to be sad. Ask the volunteer to go to the centre of the circle. Ask them to pretend to be sad. How would they act if they were really sad? While the child is pretending, ask the remaining children to chant with you:
    Sad Person, Sad Person,
    It's okay to feel like you do
    Can someone in our group
    Be kind to you?

5. The SAD PERSON is asked to point to or name someone in the group. This person goes to the bowl, selects a 'gift' and brings it to them. The SAD PERSON then returns to their place in the circle, and the child who selected and gave the gift can pretend to be the SAD PERSON. If not, the teacher can select another child. The chant and the activity are repeated.

Want to do more?
Be aware of the children who are not selected. Take a turn being the SAD PERSON and choose a child who is likely to be overlooked. Make sure every child has the opportunity to be the SAD PERSON. Never tell a child who to pick. Some children may be selected more than once. This is acceptable, but no child should have more than one turn to be the SAD PERSON.
• Read *Mufaro's Beautiful Daughters* by John Steptoe (Puffin Books).

Involving parents
Children can bring home copies of the SAD PERSON chant. Parents and children can repeat the activity at home.

The Star Seat

Encouragement

✂ ○

Age 4+

Things you will need
Sheet of felt to drape over the back of a chair
Stars of different sizes cut from yellow felt
Assorted decorations
White glue
Small chair

This activity provides a special moment of affirmation for a child. Choosing the right time and child is important. The cheers are for the child because that child is special. The cheers are not based on success. They are unconditional. Everyone is a star.

What to do
1. Drape the felt sheet across the art table and set out the decorations and glue. Tell the children that you need their help to make a blanket for a STAR SEAT. Invite them to glue the various stars and decorations onto the felt blanket.

2. When the blanket has been completed and the glue completely dried ask the children together in a circle. Drape it over the back of a small chair next to you. Tell the children that this is a STAR SEAT.

3. Ask for a volunteer to sit in the STAR SEAT. After the special person sits in the chair, mention some of the things you appreciate about that person. Invite other children to do likewise. Tell the group that you want them to cheer and clap when the person in the Star Seat gives their name. Ask the volunteer their name and start cheering. Raise your hands when you want the cheering to stop.

4. Conduct no more than two STAR SEAT cheers each time. Be sure to give every child an opportunity over a period of time.

Want to do more?
If a child makes a negative comment about someone in THE STAR SEAT, respond with something like, *Yes, that upsets you when _____ does that. But now we are thinking about the things we appreciate about _____.*

Involving parents
Parents and children can cheer each other at home. Anyone can nominate someone else in the family, or family members can ask to be cheered themselves.

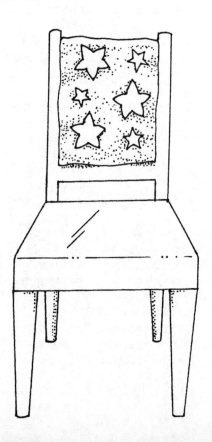

Look, No Hands

Helping, consideration for others

○

Age **4+**

Things you will need
By placing yourself in a dependent position, you empower children to help. Let other teachers or administrators know about this activity in case they stop by to visit. Be sure there is an extra helper or parent in the classroom on this day.

What to do
1. Talk with the children about the special needs of disabled people. How do we help someone who cannot see or cannot hear or cannot walk or cannot talk?

2. Tell the group you would like to see what it would be like to be a person in the class who cannot use their arms or hands. Tell them that, for the rest of the morning, you are going to wrap a bandage around your arms to bring them so close to your body that you cannot move them. Emphasize that you are pretending. You can remove the bandage at any time if you have to. You are really okay.

3. Ask the children or another teacher for help in wrapping the ace bandage around your arms so that they are held comfortably to your body.

4. Tell the children that you will need their help because you cannot use your arms or hands. Talk for a few minutes about what you may need them to do. Mention that you have a few ace bandages they can use. Emphasize that although you are going to keep your bandage on for the rest of the morning, they can remove theirs whenever they wish.

5. Call the children together when you remove the bandage. Ask for their help. Take a few moments to talk about what happened and how you felt during the experience.

Want to do more?
Try living with wrapped arms at home for about the length of time that you will have them on at school to make sure you can complete the activity. If it proves too frustrating, give up the use of only one arm and hand. Keep a few extra bandages in case children would like to handicap themselves for a short while.

Involving parents
Parents can try the same activity for a short period of time at home. Children can help with simple tasks like making lunch or tying a parent's shoes.

Know Hear

Helping, consideration for others   ○

Age **4+**

Things you will need

A comfortable device, such as a pair of earmuffs, that completely covers the ears

Although you cannot experience what it really feels like to be deaf, you can role play being a deaf person. Children will have to adjust to accommodate your loss of hearing. This activity may frustrate children anxious to tell you something while you pretend to be deaf. You may have to direct their comments to another teacher.

What to do

1. Ask children why hearing is important. Discuss how deaf people communicate through sign language and lip reading. Ask the children how other people could give them the following messages if they were deaf:
   It is time for dinner
   It is time to go to sleep
   I like you
   Goodbye

2. Tell the children you would like to find out what it would be like to be a person who cannot hear in their classroom. Ask them to listen to the sounds around them. Then ask them to cover their ears with their hands for a moment and listen. How does it feel not to hear well? Tell them you are going to cover your ears so that you cannot hear well. You are going to pretend to be deaf for the rest of the morning. You will need their help. If they want to talk to you, they will have to use their hands and bodies to tell you what they want.

3. Put on the ear covers and continue with other activities. (Yes, you will look a little silly in July.) When the children talk to you, reply, I know that you are talking to me because I see your mouth moving. I am pretending not to hear you. You will have to show me so I can see what you mean.

4. Call the children together in a circle, take off the ear covers and share your experience with the children.

Want to do more?

Ask someone who can sign to visit your class and demonstrate the skill. Your visitor can teach children a few simple statements in sign language, such as 'I love you.'
• Try dispensing with the ear covering. This situation is more realistic but potentially more confusing for children who find it difficult to remember that you are 'deaf.'
• Read *Amanda's Butterfly* by Nick Butterworth (Picture Lions).

Involving parents

Ask children to mime three messages to their parents and see if they can guess three them: 'I love you,' 'I am hungry' and 'I am happy.' Parents can create their own simple messages to sign to their children.

Gentle Breeze

Looking after others, gentleness, cooperation

◯

Age *4+*

Things you will need
Nothing

In this activity, children work together to provide a gentle, comforting experience for a classmate. This may be an excellent opportunity for a child who is overlooked and ignored by others. Do not force any child to participate.

What to do
1. Talk with children for a few moments about gentleness. How would a person be gentle to a baby, a flower or a puppy?

2. Begin the activity with the following story:

   Once upon a time in Butterberry Hill, Sam was very tired after a long day of playing with his friends. He stretched out to rest under the most beautiful tree. In just a few moments he was fast asleep. The kind tree felt sorry for Sam. Its branches gently drifted down and lifted him up to rock him back and forth. But when a storm arrived, the tree gently returned him to earth so Sam could run home. The End.

3. Ask a child to volunteer to be Sam. They lie down on their back with her arms at her sides and legs together. Ask for eight to nine children to be branches on the tree. These children kneel on both sides of the 'tired' child, where their eyes are closed. The branches slide their hands, palms up, underneath the 'tired' child's back and legs. The teacher should position herself at the child's head, securing the head, neck and upper spine.

4. On the teacher's signal, the branches slowly lift the child from the ground until they are standing. As they lift, the branches make a quiet wind sound.

5. After the child is lifted, the branches slowly rock back and forth in unison while repeating after the teacher, to the tune of *Rockabye Baby*.
   Rockabye person, in the treetops,
   When the wind blows the branches will rock,
   When the storm comes the branches will fall,
   And down comes the person, branches and all.

6. On the last line of the chant, slowly lower the child until they are resting on the ground. Ask the branches to remove their hands slowly.

7. Repeat with another volunteer as the 'tired' child.

Want to do more?
Children in my groups were quiet and serious whenever they lifted one of their classmates. If they start being silly, remind them how important it is to be gentle and careful.
• The 'tired' child can choose the 'branches' to do the lifting.

Involving parents
A mother and father working together can lift a child into the GENTLE BREEZE. During a family reunion, a group of adults can work with children to lift and rock another adult.

I'm Mobile

Helping

○ ✂

Age **4+**

Things you will need
One sheet of paper for each child
Bowl of crayons
Glue
Collage materials, in individual cups

This activity conveys to children that they can ask for as well as offer help. Requesting help is part of the social fabric of give-and-take, not a sign of weakness.

What to do

1. Set the art materials on a separate table, well away from where the group meets.

2. When the children are sitting together in a circle ask them if they know what 'help' means. Discuss various ways in which people can help each other. For example, if someone drops a bag of shopping, people nearby can help pick them up. Or, if parents have a big task to do at home, their children can help them complete it. Tell the children you have an activity for them that involves helping each other.

3. Ask the children to identify things they can do with a sheet of paper. For example, they can draw on it, cut it, paste something onto it, fold it into something and so on. Take a sheet of paper and say, *Let's pretend I am someone who cannot walk. I do not have my wheelchair with me and need your help. I would like to draw a picture on this paper. Can someone help by getting the crayons for me?* When a volunteer returns with the crayons, thank them and then draw a simple picture. Ask the volunteer to return the crayons to the art table.

4. Ask the children to choose a partner and decide who will pretend they cannot walk and who will be helpers. Hand out paper to the children who cannot walk. Ask them to think of something they would like to do with the paper. After a few moments, tell them to ask their helpers to get the materials that they need. They should bring only one type of thing at a time. When they have finished, the helpers should return the materials to the art table. After a while, the partners should switch roles. Tell the children that they can complete their projects after the group has finished meeting.

5. When both partners have had the opportunity to ask and receive help, summarize the activity by saying,

Sometimes we really like to get help from other people, and sometimes we like to be helpful. Give examples of children who helped. Then say, *Sometimes we don't want help, and sometimes we don't feel like helping. Everyone needs help at some time, though. Helping others who need our help is important.*

Want to do more?
Make a chart with children's names and a list of repetitive tasks that need to be performed in the classroom. Assign simple work roles to children on a weekly basis on the chart.

Involving parents
Ask parents to look for opportunities to ask children for help even if they do not really need it, for example, washing dishes or opening a door when the parent's arms are full.

The Night Train, p.179

Giving Free   ◯

Generosity   *Age* 5+

Things you will need
A bag of small, nutritious biscuits (about as many as there are children in the group)

This activity should be conducted only after a snack or meal. Recognize children's spontaneous generosity. Giving is based on feeling comfortable and secure with what is owned. Do not force children to give what they want to keep. Emphasize the pleasure to be gained by doing something kind and respond positively to their efforts.

What to do
1. Tell the children you have a giving activity for them to do. Take out the bag of biscuits and say, *Here is a bag of biscuits that I am going to give to someone in the group. When this person gets the bag, they may decide to keep them all, give them all away, or give some away and keep some. When they have finished, we will talk about what happened.*

2. Give the bag to one of the children, choosing a typically generous child the first time you introduce this activity. When they have finished with the bag, ask the children who received biscuits to raise their hands. Talk about how they feel. Ask those who did not receive anything to raise their hands and encourage them to say how they feel.

3. Try to help the children understand that sometimes other people will not want to give things to them. Explain that they may feel sad since it is hard to be left out. Tell them that if they are patient, and if they ask nicely, they may find that someone will be generous.

Want to do more?
Give two bags simultaneously to two different children.
• Or begin the activity by choosing the shyest or most isolated child in the group to give out the biscuits.
• Read *Mr Grumpy's Outing* by John Burningham (Puffin Books).

Involving parents
Parents can encourage generosity by helping their children gather old, unneeded toys and clothes to give to charity. Parents can demonstrate their own generosity by giving personal belongings to others and discussing their reasons with their children.

Night Train

○ ✤

Helping, protection, cooperation

Age **5+**

Things you will need
Extra belts or ropes cut to serve as belts
Three hats
Three blindfolds

NIGHT TRAIN combines three different but complementary skills. The engine has to protect the cars as it moves through the forest, while the trees provide warnings. The engine and cars have to cooperate to remain intact as the whole train moves. The train is delivering the toys to help children in the town.

What to do
1. Tell the children that they are going to pretend to be a train bringing toys for children who live in a town on the other side of a forest. But this train is moving at night, and only the engine has a light to see.

2. Ask for a volunteer to be the engine and three others to be the train cars. The remaining children are trees in the forest. Leave enough room between the trees to ensure safety. Tell the trees that they are not to move. They can make an 'oooo' sound if any train car is about to bump into them. Place hats on three of the trees. Tell the engine they must go around the trees with hats before they can leave the forest.

3. The cars line up behind the engine and hold onto the belt of the person in front of them. Provide belts or a loop of rope if necessary. When the train is ready, blindfold each of the cars. Emphasize that the engine should move slowly. Supervise closely.

4. Stand on the other side of the forest and tell the train that you are the town they have to reach. Ask them to begin.

5. Let the children take turns being the engine.

Want to do more?
To increase the challenge, operate two trains at the same time (if you have enough children), add more cars to the engine and/or bring the trees more closely together. Increasing the difficulty requires closer supervision.
• You may also conduct the activity without blindfolds in a darkened room or outside at night. Give the engine a torch.

Involving parents
Parents and children can take turns being the engine for a FAMILY TRAIN that chugs around the house. The train cars can be blindfolded as described above. If a young child is the engine, one adult should not be blindfolded so that they can act as a guardian.

Dream Catcher

Generosity

○ ✂

Age *5+*

Things you will need
Wool, string or embroidery thread
A hoop made of plastic, wood or metal

Keep in mind that sharing distinctly differs from giving. Sharing means the temporary loss of a personal belonging that is eventually returned. Giving means giving up the object forever. Avoid confusing the two when talking to children. For example, you give a biscuit to someone, but you share your truck.

What to do
1. Before conducting this activity, make your own DREAM CATCHER to show the children.

2. Talk with the children about dreams and nightmares. Describe some of your experiences as a child. Show them the DREAM CATCHER you have made and discuss the Native American custom of using DREAM CATCHERS to prevent nightmares. The spider's web DREAM CATCHER is hung near the bed to catch bad dreams as

they pass through. Good dreams always find a way through the holes in the web. The traditional Native American DREAM CATCHER was made with a circle of willow branches tied with grasses or reed. The design was woven with grasses or raffia.

3. Tell the children they can make a DREAM CATCHER to give to someone they would like to help sleep more comfortably. In the art area, help them through the steps to create their own DREAM CATCHER:

STEP 1. Tie your thread (or whatever material you have chosen to use) onto the edge of the hoop.

STEP 2. Loop the yarn under and then over the edge of the hoop at desired intervals. The closer you space the yarn, the finer the web will be. Pull it tightly after each loop until you have circled back to the first loop.

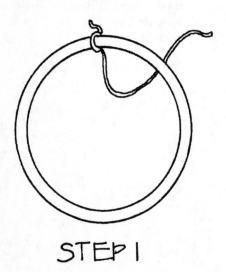

STEP 1

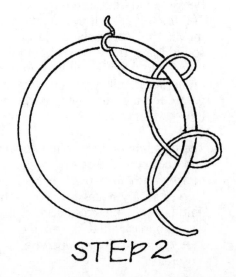

STEP 2

STEP 3. Now loop your yarn under and over the centre of each loop as shown in the illustration. Continue threading the thread through the centres until you reach the middle.

STEP 4. Pull tight and tie off. You now have a simplified version of the Native American DREAM CATCHER.

4. When they give their DREAM CATCHERS to another person, children should tell them about the Native American custom of hanging these webs near the bed to catch bad dreams.

Want to do more?
If looping the thread is too difficult, simply crisscross around the hoop to form a simple web.

Involving parents
Parents and children can make DREAM CATCHERS to give to each other.

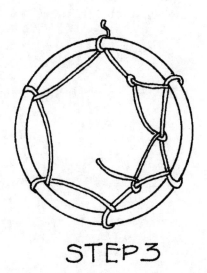

STEP3

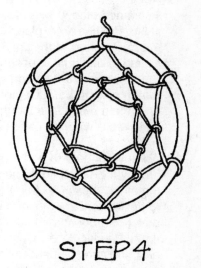

STEP4

Sprain Pain

Looking after others, gentleness, consideration of others   Age 5+

○

Things you will need
One bandage for every two children

Keep in mind that the focus of this activity is the effort to give and receive help, not accurate medical care.

What to do
1. Ask the children if they have ever had a sprained ankle or elbow. Explain what happens when someone has a sprain.

2. Ask for a volunteer to pretend to have a sprained elbow, wrist, knee or ankle. Provide an explanation for the injury. A sprain of the ankle, for example, might have occurred while running across a field and catching a foot in a small hole. Demonstrate how to drape the bandage around the joint and secure with the metal tabs.

3. Ask the children to find a partner. One will be the injured person and the other, the carer. Ask the partners to decide which of them has the pretend injury and where they were injured: ankle, knee, wrist or elbow. Give the carers a bandage and ask them to wrap the injured person's joint. Provide assistance where needed.

4. When they have finished, switch roles to give everyone an opportunity to help.

Want to do more?
Simplify the activity by shortening the length of the bandage and assisting helpers with the wrapping.
• Read *Mr Dog* by Babette Cole (Red Fox).

Involving parents
Ask parents to lend you bandages to reduce expenses. Parents can role play the injured person at home, and children provide the first aid.

Say Something Nice

Encouragement   Age 5+

Things you will need
Nothing

The purpose of this activity is to provide practice in giving compliments. Even though the situation created is artificial, SAY SOMETHING NICE reinforces a goal of kindness and spontaneous support.

What to do
1. Begin the activity by saying, *Sometimes we find it difficult to tell other people what we like about them. Can you tell me something you like about your mothers? About your fathers? Let's think about what we like about others in our class.* Discuss the meaning of the word 'compliment.' Would anyone like to hear what others like about them?

2. When a child volunteers, say, *Chris would like to hear what we like about him. I will start. 'Chris, I like your bright smile when you come to class in the morning. That smile really cheers me up.'* The statement you make should be clear, specific and honest: *I like the way you try to help other children when they can't do something; if I need help I know I can count on you,* is better than *You are nice to other people.*

3. After you finish, invite other children to describe what they like about the person receiving compliments. If someone voices a complaint, you can respond, Yes, that is something you want to tell Chris, but this is a time for talking about what we like about others. Dan, what does Chris do that you like? If a child cannot think of anything, introduce a few of your observations about this child's relationship with the volunteer. *Dan, you really seem to get on well with Chris when you ride bikes together. Do you like being with Chris when you play on the bikes? Is that true?*

4. To avoid wordiness, focus on only one volunteer each time you initiate this activity.

Want to do more?
Begin by asking the children to say what they like about you.
• Or, after several comments, ask the children being complimented to identify something they like about themselves. As children become more comfortable complimenting others, this activity can shift entirely to identifying personal strengths.
• Children who cannot think of complimentary things to say to others are good candidates for receiving compliments.

Involving parents
Parents can involve children in spontaneous 'strength bombardment.' One family member begins by giving a compliment or expressing appreciation to another. Others follow with their own supportive comments to the family member who spoke first.

Taste Helpers

Helping, gentleness

○ 🍒

Age 5+

Things you will need
Bowls of yoghurt, jelly and fruit salad
Bag of wooden or plastic spoons (about four per child)
Paper cup with water for each child
Blindfold

Although this activity is described to children as a guessing game, the primary emphasis is the gentle and helpful behaviour children offer while feeding their partners. It also provides a safe situation for children to wear a blindfold. Check for food allergies before engaging in any activity involving food.

What to do
1. When they have gathered in a circle tell the children you have a guessing game for them to play with a partner in the snack area. One partner wears a blindfold, and the other selects one of three foods to feed the blindfolded partner.

2. Set out bowls, spoons and cups of water. Invite the children to find a partner.

3. Partners should sit close together, facing each other. After sitting, the child who will taste the food should be gently blindfolded. Partners take a spoon and decide what to give the blindfolded child. Emphasize the gentleness needed for feeding.

4. After carefully tasting what their partner has selected, the children guess what it is.

5. After tasting the three types of food, the partners switch roles.

6. Ask the children to take their time. They should taste the food carefully before guessing and drink water between samples. They should use a clean spoon each time.

Want to do more?
Make the activity more challenging by increasing the number of foods. Add variety by changing the types of foods. For example, offer five or six different types of raw vegetables or fruits.
• Read *Oliver's Vegetables* by Vivian French, illustrated by Alison Bartlett (Hodder Children's Books).

Involving parents
Parents can repeat the activity at home. For example, one parent can select food for a child to feed the other blindfolded parent.

Touch Me   ○ ◆●

Gentleness   *Age* 5+

Things you will need
Collect an assortment of objects with textured surfaces: furry cloth, sandpaper, crumpled piece of paper, smooth stone, rubber ball, silk.

Children are challenged to touch another person's face in a way that their partners will experience as gentle and sensitive. Children who choose to be blindfolded show trust in their partner's kindness.

What to do
1. When they are gathered in a circle, show the children the tray of objects. See whether they can identify each one. Tell them you have a guessing game for them to play in the science area. One partner puts on a blindfold. The other partner gently touches the blindfolded child's face with an object. The blindfolded partner then guesses what is touching her skin.

2. Place the tray of objects on a table. Invite the children to find a partner. Supervise closely.

3. Partners should sit close together, facing each other. Once seated, the child to be touched is gently blindfolded. Partners choose an object and then gently touch it to their partner's cheek with it. Emphasize gentleness. Demonstrate touching and supervise to ensure safe and gentle behaviour.

4. After thoughtfully considering the object's texture, the children guess its identity.

5. After three or four objects, partners switch roles.

6. Encourage the children to take their time to feel the object rather than rush to guess its identity.

Want to do more?
Increase the challenge by adding more objects.
• Decrease the challenge by asking the children to place the objects in their partners' hands.
• Read *Dads Are Such Fun* by Jacqueline Wood, illustrated by Rog Bonner (All Books for Children).

Involving parents
Parents can repeat the activity at home, taking turns with their children to be blindfolded.

Roly-Poly and the Kind Fairies   ○ ✿

Helping, rescue, gentleness, consideration for others   Age 5+

Things you will need
Blindfolds
Timer
Two 7 m (22') lengths of rope or twine
Large blanket or sheet

Young children have problems guiding others safely because of their egocentrism. They use their own point of view to avoid obstacles, but are less likely to see through the eyes of those they guide. They may pass safely under the branch of a tree without realizing that it will catch the taller, blindfolded person they are guiding. This activity challenges children to consider the point of view of others.

What to do
1. With the two lengths of rope or twine, mark off the boundaries of a path about one metre/three feet wide and at least 7 m (22') long. This is the bridge. Place a large blanket or sheet at one end of the bridge to be the 'island.'

2. Introduce the activity when the children have gathered in a   circle with the following story:

Once upon a time near Butterberry Hill, there was a terrible fire on an island in Moonmist Lake. All the animals on the island were in great danger. They tried to run away but there was no place to go. A long and narrow rock bridge provided the only escape off the island. But the animals were afraid. There was a lot of smoke, and the night was dark. They could not see at all to cross the bridge. The water was too deep to swim. Roly-Poly the Bear prayed for someone to help him and his friends. As the flames grew closer and closer, he felt someone kind and gentle take him by the arm. I am your friend, your protector, he heard a Kind Fairy say. Even though they could not see where they were going, Roly-Poly and his friends were led safely across the bridge by the Kind Fairies. The End.

3. Tell the children you have a game in which they can try to give the protection and help that Roly-Poly received. Point to the path and tell them that it is the bridge. At one end is the island and at the other end, safety.

4. Half of the children volunteer to be animals, the other half, Kind Fairies. Tell them that, because the animals cannot see in the dark and smoke, they will be blindfolded and led across the bridge to safety by the Kind Fairies. Once the blindfolds are on, start the timer. The object of the game is to lead all the animals across the bridge before the timer goes off. Helpers should be careful not to let the animals walk over the boundaries of the bridge. Demonstrate how to lead a blindfolded person gently.

5. After helping the animals put on their blindfolds, ask them what kind of animal they would like to be. Give each child a helper to guide them across the bridge.

6. Once the animals have been led to safety, they may remove their blindfolds and switch roles with their rescuers. When everyone has had a turn, talk about the rescue.

Want to do more?

For an additional challenge, add sharp curves to the path, increase its length or make it narrower.

• Shorten the amount of time to make the rescue.

• Read *Davy's Scary Journey* by Christine Leeson, illustrated by Tim Warnes (Magi Publications).

Involving parents

Parents can play a similar game with their children. For the island, use a bed, and for the bridge, large sheets folded and stretched end-to-end on the floor. Parents and children can take turns being ROLY-POLY AND THE KIND FAIRIES.

No Walk   ○

Helping, consideration for others   Age 5+

Things you will need
Bandage
Crutches or wheelchair (optional)

Make sure that adult assistance is
available. Activities that temporarily
disable your senses or ability to move
have three complementary goals: to
challenge children to adjust their
expectations in order to help, to provide
the teacher with a personal experience
of physical disability, and to strengthen
relationships between teacher and
children.

What to do
1. Contact a local health centre,
   describe the activity you hope to do
   with your class and ask whether they
   would lend what you need for the
   day.

2. Talk with the children about the
   special needs of disabled people.
   How do we help someone who
   cannot see or hear or walk or talk?

3. Tell the group you want to see what it
   would be like to be a person in the
   class who cannot walk. Tell them that
   for the rest of the class day, you will
   wear a bandage wrapped around your
   legs so that you cannot move your
   legs or feet. Emphasize that you will
   be pretending to not be able to walk.
   You could remove the bandage at any
   time if necessary.

4. Wrap the bandage around your ankles
   to hold them comfortably together.

5. Tell the children that you will need
   their help because you cannot walk.
   Talk for a few minutes about what

you may need them to do. Mention
that you have other ace bandages that
they could use to wrap their ankles,
too. Emphasize that although you are
going to wear your bandage the rest
of the morning, they can wear theirs
for as long as they want.

6. Getting around is going to be a
   problem. You may use crutches or a
   wheelchair or crawl as best you can.
   If you need to go outside, you will
   need the crutches or wheelchair.
   Arrange with another adult to carry
   the wheelchair outside, if necessary.

7. Provide supervision for children
   wearing bandages, especially if they
   need to go up or down stairs.

8. Call the children together. Take a few
   moments to talk about what happened
   and how you felt during the
   experience. Point out ways in which
   they helped you.

Want to do more?
Combine handicaps to increase the
challenge. How would children respond
to someone who cannot see or walk, or
cannot hear or talk?
• Read *The Frightened Little Owl* by
Mark Ezra, illustrated by Gavin Rowe
(Magi Publications).

Involving parents
Parents can take their children for a
walk around the house and point out the
problems that a person confined to a
wheelchair might have living there. They
can explore the surrounding community
to identify the physical barriers and
other problems a person in a wheelchair
would face.

Cats and Mice

○ ❀

Gentleness

Age 5+

Things you will need
Red and yellow construction paper
Tape
Scissors
Music

Children may have to be reminded to be gentle during this activity. If you find yourself continually correcting them, simplify the activity. Some children are uncomfortable with intensive physical contact.

What to do
1. Cut strips of red and yellow construction paper. Tape the strips together to make child-size headbands. Cut circles from the yellow paper and triangles from the red. Attach two circles to the yellow bands to make enough mouse ears for half the children. Add the triangles to the red bands to make enough cat ears for all the children, minus one.

2. Introduce the game of CATS AND MICE to the children. In this game, cats do not eat mice — they hug them. To begin, the children are divided equally into cats and mice. Give the cats a red headband and the mice a yellow headband. When the music begins to play, the mice and cats walk around the room, squeaking or meowing. When the music stops, the cats must find a mouse to hug gently. Cats may hug each other, but must have at least one mouse in their 'hug bunch.'

3. After the cats and mice hug briefly, choose one mouse to become a cat. Take this child's mouse headband and replace it with a cat headband. Start the music and continue as before.

4. Continue adding cats to the group until you only have one mouse left. When the music stops, everyone will be in one big group hug around one mouse.

Want to do more?
Play a cat yourself and seek out mice that need a hug.

Involving parents
Parents can play a game of HUDDLE HUG with their children. At any time, one family member will announce, I need a huddle hug. Everyone immediately runs to that family member to crowd together to give him a hug.

Night Flying

Helping, rescue, consideration for others

○ ✿

Age 5+

Things you will need
Blindfold
Small blanket

For this activity, the children must understand such movement commands such as turn left, turn right, move forward, turn around and stop. Be sure the room is entirely free of clutter. Allow children to remove the blindfolds at any time. If there is another adult in the classroom, demonstrate the activity before the children begin.

What to do
1. Begin the activity with the following story:

   Once upon a time near Butterberry Hill, a small aeroplane was trying to land at the airport. But the night was dark, and the lights on the runway were not working. Amy's dad was in the control tower. He could see the plane on his radar, so he got on the radio and told the pilot what direction to fly in order to land on the runway. The people on the plane were very happy when they arrived safely. The End.

2. Tell the children you have a game for them to play about flying at night. One person will be like Amy's dad, guiding another person who will be blindfolded and pretends to be the aeroplane. The helper guides the aeroplane from one side of the room to a small blanket on the other side. The helper guides only by telling the plane where to go.

3. The children must be sufficiently mature to understand how to turn right and turn left. Ask the children to stand and gather in a group behind you. Lead them through the directions with their eyes open. Turn left, stop, turn right, stop, turn around. Say the directions out loud as you move. Invite one child to stand in front of the group and give them directions.

4. Spread a small blanket on one side of the room. This is the airport. Take out a blindfold and ask if anyone would like to try the activity with a partner. The partners will have to decide between them who will be the guide and who will be the aeroplane.

5. Put the blindfold on the plane. When ready, the guide can begin directing the plane to the airport. He can accompany the plane but should not physically direct the partner. The teacher should remain close by to ensure safety.

6. Upon arriving at the blanket, the guide may tell the plane to sit down and remove the blindfold.

7. Repeat the activity, switching roles.

Want to do more?
Children who have difficulty giving verbal directions can stand behind their partners and gently guide them toward the goal, telling them when they arrive.
• Children who are proficient in this activity can try Drop in the Bucket.
• To increase difficulty, try having more than one aeroplane or setting a timer (for a few minutes) to indicate when the aeroplane runs out of fuel.

• To decrease difficulty, try the activity without blindfolds. Whisper to the guide an object or location for the aeroplane to fly to. The guide then directs the aeroplane without specifically mentioning the goal.
• Read *The Way Home* by Judith Benét Richardson (Red Fox).

Involving parents
Parents can repeat the activity at home.

Parachute Rescue

Rescue, cooperation

✳

Age *5+*

Things you will need
Lightweight fabric cut into 30 cm (12")
squares (like handkerchiefs)
String
Scissors
Small, safe and fairly light objects to
serve as weights (a plastic spool works
well)
Small plastic buckets or similar
containers

Watch out for collisions if the children
are throwing more than one parachute at
a time.

What to do
1. Attach four strings of identical length
   to each corner of the fabric and
   connect the free ends to the weight.

2. Roll the parachute into a ball, keeping
   the weight free. Practise throwing the
   parachute until it opens properly.

3. Gather the children into a circle near
   a large grassy area outside. Show the
   parachute and tell them you have a
   rescue game for them to play. Take a
   few moments to explore their ideas
   about 'rescuing.' Tell them that a jet's
   engine has broken down, and the
   pilot had to eject before the plane
   crashed. Unfortunately (gesture
   toward the grass), the plane was over
   the ocean. The object of the game is
   to rescue the parachuting pilot before
   he hits the water.

4. The children work in pairs to make
   the rescue. Emphasize cooperation.
   Each pair has a parachute and a
   bucket. One child throws the
   parachute while the other tries to
   rescue it by catching it with the

bucket. Show the children how to
throw and catch the parachute. If the
parachute lands in the water, the
rescuer should run to it as fast as
possible.

5. Children should be encouraged to
   take turns being a rescuer.

Want to do more?
Since the emphasis is on rescuing, you
can do all the throwing yourself.
• More than one parachute can be
thrown to a rescuer.
• Read *The Enchanted Wood* by Ruth
Sanderson (Little, Brown).

Involving parents
Parents can play PARACHUTE RESCUE
outside with their children.

Forest Tag

Encouragement, rescue, gentleness

Age 5+

Things you will need
Small circles of yellow felt
Cardboard box

A game with several rules is easier when played in a dramatic context.

What to do
1. Gather in a circle and introduce the rescue adventure with the following story:

   Once upon a time, there was a great treasure on the other side of Bluestone Forest. Many tried to find the treasure and bring it back to Butterberry Hill. Unfortunately, the trees of this forest were magic. Anyone who touched their branches would be turned to stone like a statue. The End.

2. Ask the children if they would like to get the great treasure. Show them a handful of small felt circles (the treasure). Ask for about five volunteers to try to rescue the treasure from the other side of the forest. The rest of the children are trees. (You need at least a dozen trees.)

3. Evenly distribute the trees throughout the forest. Place them fairly close to each other, but their 'branches' should not touch even when they stretch. Tell the trees that they can bend and twist, but their feet cannot move at all. They must stay in one spot.

4. Put the gold chest (cardboard box) on one side of the forest and the pieces of gold on the other. The rescuers start from a spot near the gold chest. Emphasize that if a tree touches them,

they will be turned to stone. Any child who reaches the gold can return to a stone child and free them with a gentle hug, so long as they avoid the touch of the trees. Once they have been free children can try again to retrieve the gold. Children who reach the gold may take one piece and try to return it to the gold chest. They can keep trying until all the gold has been returned, or all the rescuers have been turned to stone.

Want to do more?
Spread out the trees to make the passage easier.
• Clump them together to make it more difficult.
• Read *Ronnie the Red-eyed Tree Frog* by Martin and Tanis Jordan (Kingfisher Books).

Involving parents
Ask parents to think of fairy tales that have a rescue theme, like The Snow Queen and Sleeping Beauty. They can look for one of these stories at the local library to read and discuss with their children.

Mrs Hen

Helping, protect/rescue

Things you will need
Approximately three sheets of scrap paper per child
Paper bag or box

If children seem confused by activities that include several distinct roles and goals, look for ways to make them more understandable. Use visual cues to help children remember who is doing what. Mrs Hen, for example, can wear a fancy flower hat and Mr Fox, a wool cap. Put whiskers on the fox with make-up or cut a headband with pointed ears out of construction paper.

What to do
1. Make 'eggs' by crumpling the sheets of paper into balls.

2. Gather the children into a circle and tell them the story about poor Mrs Hen.

   Once upon a time in Butterberry Hill, someone stole into the hen house and took all of Mrs Hen's eggs and hid them in the farmyard. She wants to get them back. But only her Baby Chicks can retrieve her eggs and return them to the nest. Mr Fox will try to stop them. Can Mrs Hen protect her Baby Chicks while they help her rescue her eggs? The End.

3. One child volunteers to be Mrs Hen and one to be Mr Fox. The rest of the children are Baby Chicks. The object of the game is for the chicks to bring their mother's eggs back to her nest without being caught by a fox. Any fox who tags a chick says, 'Shazaam!' That chick then becomes a fox. Chicks cannot be caught if they are

hugging (not just touching) Mrs Hen. Only Baby Chicks can bring the eggs back to the nest, but they can only pick up an egg when they are not hugging Mrs Hen.

4. Set Mrs Hen's nest (the paper bag or box) in the middle of the play area. Disperse her eggs throughout the play area. Ask Mrs Hen and her chicks to gather around the nest. Tell Mr Fox to go to the outer edge of the play area.

5. Announce, *Okay, Baby Chicks get Mrs Hen's eggs!* At that moment, Mr Fox can try to catch any Baby Chicks who are not hugging Mrs Hen. The game ends when all the eggs have been returned to the nest, or more likely, all the chicks have been turned into foxes.

6. After the group has played a couple of times, relax for a few moments. Talk with the children about helping and protecting.

Want to do more?
The first few times you play, you can be Mr Fox to help the children learn the rules.
• With older children, trying adding a Mr Rooster and a second Mr Fox. Play by the same rules, but in this version, Mr Rooster can catch a fox and say *'Zap!'* When that happens, the fox becomes a chick. Like Mrs Hen, Mr Rooster cannot be changed into a fox.
• It may help to have Mrs Hen and Mr Rooster wear different hats.
• Read *The Rescue Party* by Nick Butterworth (HarperCollins).

Involving parents
Encourage children and parents to play rescue and helping games at home. A chair can become a boat in a lake of crocodiles. Pretend the boat is sinking, and the children have to rescue the parents.

Missing Person, p.40

Farmer Brown and the Rabbits ○ ❀ △ ✳

Protection   *Age* 5+

Things you will need
Three large paper bags
Carrots cut from orange felt
Simple headbands for the rabbits cut
from construction paper
A hat for Farmer Brown

Every activity has at least one role that is
critical to its success. That role is often
the most difficult to understand. Farmer
Brown is the key role here. When
children first try this activity, you can
play FARMER BROWN This will also
enable you to control the tempo.

What to do
1. When the children have gathered in a
   circle tell them the story of Farmer
   Brown and the Rabbits.

   Once upon a time, a farmer by the
   name of Farmer Brown lived just
   outside of Butterberry Hill. Farmer
   Brown's favourite food in the whole
   world was carrots. He loved sliced
   and buttered carrots, crunchy carrots
   with a little salt, carrot pie and carrot
   juice. So one spring he planted a
   whole garden of carrots. He watered
   his garden every day and made sure
   no weeds grew. Finally, the carrots
   were ready to harvest. Farmer Brown
   harvested all the carrots he could eat
   (show the children the 'carrots').
   Unfortunately, Briarbutton and his
   hungry rabbit friends knew all about
   those carrots, too. So when Farmer
   Brown was not looking, they grabbed
   his carrots and hopped away as fast as
   they could. Poor Farmer Brown. He
   chased the rabbits, but when
   Briarbutton and his friends hid behind
   a tree, he could not find them. The
   End.

2. Say to the children: *Let's play a game.
   I will be Farmer Brown. Who would
   like to pretend to be the rabbits?*
   Choose three children to be
   Briarbutton and his rabbit friends. The
   rest of the children will be the trees
   that protect the rabbits.

3. Take three paper bags and set them
   on the outer edge of the play area.
   These are the rabbit holes. Spread the
   carrots on the ground in the centre of
   the circle. Spread trees throughout the
   play area. The rabbits put on
   headbands and take their positions by
   their holes. Farmer Brown puts on a
   hat and stands near the carrots.

4. The rabbits have to go to the garden,
   grab one carrot at a time and then run
   to put it into their holes. If Farmer
   Brown tags a rabbit, he gets to take
   and keep the carrot — if the rabbit
   had one. The rabbit who was tagged
   has to return immediately to their hole
   before re-entering the forest to get
   another carrot. Trees protect the
   rabbits. Rabbits are safe from Farmer
   Brown as long as they hug a tree. The
   trees must stand in one place and not
   walk around.

5. Once the rules are understood, allow
   the children to play the role of Farmer
   Brown.

Want to do more?
Make the activity easer for Farmer
Brown by increasing the number of
farmers who can catch the rabbits.
• Increase the number of rabbits to
make their task easier.

Involving parents
Parents can ask their children about their
favourite foods and how they like them
prepared.

Princess (or Prince) Gentle

Rescue, gentleness

Things you will need

Identical hats or construction paper headbands for the Mean Trolls, a different hat or headband (a crown, perhaps) for the Gentle Princess (or Prince)

Activities that involve determining a winner or completing a project have an obvious conclusion. You know when to stop. Many of the activities in this book, however, because they have purposes other than winning, do not have obvious endings. Be sensitive to the group's energy level. Finish games before fatigue or monotony sets in.

What to do

1. When the children have gathered in a circle tell them the story about the Meanies:

   Once upon a time, in a land faraway, there were Mean Trolls. People didn't like them because their touch would freeze you like a statue. People were sad to be frozen because then they couldn't move around. They couldn't eat or laugh or play. Sometimes more than one Mean Troll was running around freezing people. They thought it was funny to freeze people. Fortunately, a Gentle Princess came to town. Every time the Gentle Princess hugged someone who was frozen, they could move again. The Gentle Princess could not be frozen by a Mean Troll's touch. Did the Gentle Princess save the town? Let's find out. The End.

2. Ask for two children to volunteer to be Mean Trolls and one child to be the Gentle Princess (or Prince). Give the three children distinctive hats or headbands to remind other children of their roles.

3. The game is played like tag except that when children are tagged by Mean Trolls, they are frozen until the Gentle Princess hugs them. This has to be a gentle hug with both arms around the frozen person, not a casual touch. Once frozen children are hugged, they can move again. The Mean Trolls try to freeze everyone in the group.

4. Demonstrate the hug and emphasize how important it is to be very gentle.

5. Mark off the boundaries of the play area. Ask those pretending to be Mean Trolls to start on one side and the Gentle Princess, on the other. The rest of the children begin in the centre. Play ends after a few minutes or when everyone except the Gentle Princess has been frozen.

Want to do more?

Change the balance of the game by increasing the play area or adding Meanies or Gentle Princesses.

• With older children, consider increasing the number of Meanies and adding a rule that their freezing powers can be taken away if they are caught by the Gentle Princesses. They then become normal people who can be frozen by Mean Trolls.

• Read *The Little Troll* by Thomas Berger, illustrated by Ronald Heuninck (Floris Books).

Involving parents

Encourage parents to talk with their children about times when they were scared and the people who helped them handle whatever frightened them.

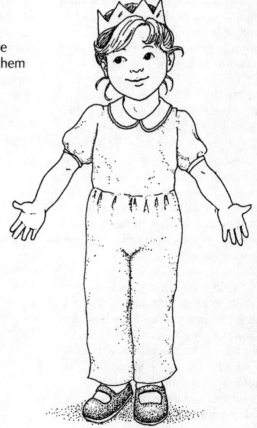

Left Out

○

Generosity, consideration for others, negotiation   Age 5+

Things you will need
One nutritious biscuit for every two children

This activity challenges children to manage scarcity. Avoid making a big fuss over children who do not receive any biscuits from others. Some children will take this mild oversight in their stride. If you act as though they should be angry or sad, however, they may become upset. Do not force or emotionally pressurize children to give their biscuits to others.

What to do
1. After the children have washed their hands, pass a biscuit to every other child sitting in the circle. Take one for yourself. Ask the children not to eat the biscuit until you tell them they can. Ask those who have a biscuit to raise their hands. Tell these children that they can choose to be kind and generous to those who did not receive biscuits.

2. Ask those who did not receive biscuits to raise their hands. Then say, Some children do not have biscuits. Would anyone like to give some of their biscuit to one of them? Wait for the children to be generous. Ask for children who still do not have a biscuit to raise their hands once more. Repeat your invitation. After this second opportunity, break your biscuit into enough pieces to give to those who received nothing from other children.

Want to do more?
To increase the challenge, reduce the number of children receiving a biscuit to a third of your group.
• Read *Something Else* by Kathryn Cave, illustrated by Chris Riddell (Penguin Books Ltd).

Involving parents
Encourage parents to try a similar activity when their child has a visitor, giving one biscuit to their child and setting another one aside. Parents can encourage their child to give part of the biscuit to the visitor. If the child refuses, they should give the other biscuit to the visitor.

Index

Games Index

Earthwise

Environmental crafts and activities with young children

Carol Petrash

Earthwise offers a year-round programme of practical ideas for encouraging young children to be aware of their environment. Written out of long experience with kindergarten groups, *Earthwise* presents a rich and varied selection of nature crafts and seasonal activities for younger children.

The fully illustrated activities are carefully graded in difficulty so that children will learn how to play safely with the elements of earth, air fire and water. They will develop knowledge and respect for Nature, the living Earth and its creatures.

Children learn about their dependence on the Earth's produce (by taking stalks of wheat and turning them into bread-flour); how to create and not just consume (by making their own gifts); how to make butter and grow food (even in the city) and how to make outdoor playhouses from natural materials.

There are seasonal suggestions for making a more earth-friendly home and classroom and also a comprehensive list of resources and suppliers.

Carol Petrash has over fifteen years experience in teaching pre-school children. She has been active in environmental projects for many years, including organic gardening and waste-recycling.

Floris Books